Route 66 Travel Guide 2025

Experience Beautiful Sites And Landmarks With Colorful Towns And Diverse Terrain In America's Cherished Highway

Toni Myles

Copyright

© 2024 Toni Myles. All rights reserved. No part of this publication may be reproduced, distributed, or transmitted in any form or by any means, including photocopying, recording, or other electronic or mechanical methods, without the prior written permission of the publisher, except in the case of brief quotations embodied in critical reviews and certain other noncommercial uses permitted by copyright law.

Table of Content

Chapter 1. Introduction... 6
    Welcome to Route 66..6
Chapter 2. Planning Your Trip............................... 8
    Best Time to Travel...8
    A Must-have Packing List..9
    Budgeting and Costs..10
Chapter 3. Route 66 Overview............................. 14
    The Route's History and Evolution...............................14
    Key Landmarks and Attractions................................... 16
Chapter 4. Regional Highlights........................... 34
    Illinois... 34
    Missouri.. 39
    Kansas... 44
    Oklahoma... 47
    Texas...53
    New Mexico..56
    Arizona... 59
    California.. 61
Chapter 5. Historical Sites and Museums............... 65
    Route 66 Museums.. 65
    Historical Markers and Monuments Along Route 66....... 69
Chapter 6. Dining and Local Eats..........................75
    Iconic Diners and Cafes.. 75
    Regional Specialties and Local Favorites.....................80
Chapter 7. Accommodation Options....................... 87
    Classic Motels and Hotels... 87
    Unique Places to Stay on Route 66.............................. 93
Chapter 8. Outdoor Adventures........................... 99
    Scenic Drives and Natural Attractions........................ 99

    Parks and Recreational Areas..104
Chapter 9. Local Culture and Festivals................... 109
    Annual Events and Celebrations......................................109
    Cultural Highlights Along Route 66................................113
Chapter 10. Practical Information........................119
    Navigational Hints...119
    Safety and Local Etiquette... 123
Conclusion...127

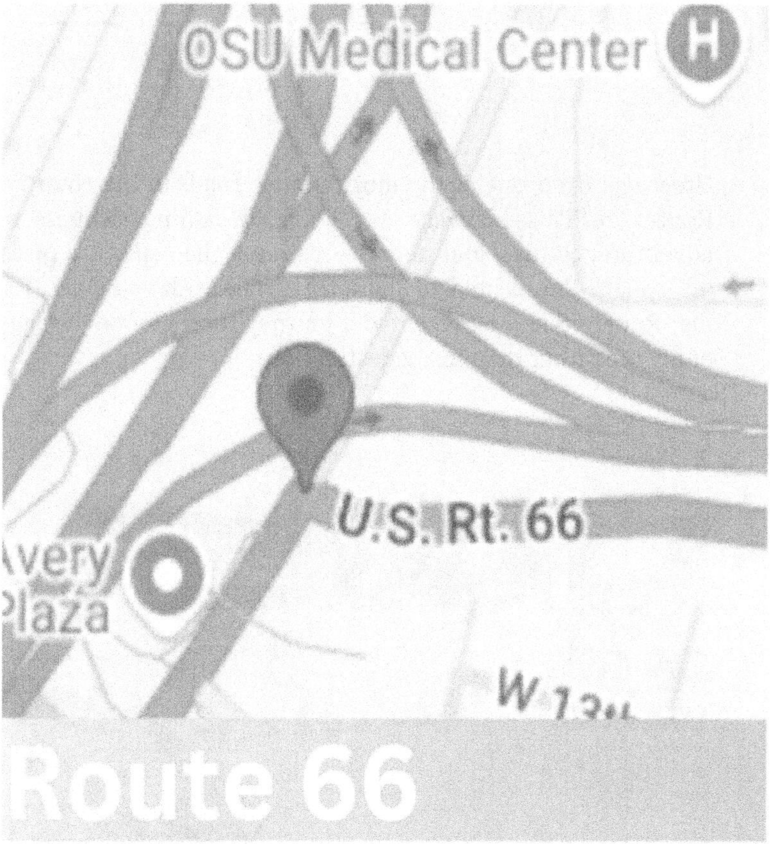

[Map image showing OSU Medical Center, U.S. Rt. 66, Avery Plaza, W 13... with "Route 66" label]

Scan the QR code

1. Open Camera: Launch your smartphone's camera app.
2. Position QR Code: Place the QR code within the camera's viewfinder.
3. Hold Steady: Keep the device steady for the camera to focus.
4. Wait for Scan: Wait for the code to be recognized.
5. Tap Notification: Follow the prompt to access the content.

Chapter 1. Introduction

Welcome to Route 66

Greetings from one of the most famous roads in the country, Route 66. This highway is a living, breathing richness of adventure, culture, and history—it's more than simply a piece of asphalt. I'm excited to share this guide with you since, for me, Route 66 has represented a journey through many stages of my life rather than just a destination.

Years ago, I was excited to find a piece of American history when I first went out on Route 66. All I had with me was a road map and a curious heart as I traveled the entire distance. From the busy streets of Chicago to the peaceful California deserts, every mile brought a fresh experience and a new tale. I visited oddball museums, paused at wayside eateries, and marveled at enduring landmarks.

However, my connection with Route 66 didn't stop there. I've had the chance to reside in a few of the places along the way over the years. I've seen the ebb and flow of life in these special places, experienced the shifting of the seasons, and strolled the same streets that tourists have been exploring for decades. Every time I went back, I discovered something fresh—a communal festival, a rediscovered monument, or a hidden treasure that I had never seen before.

Route 66 has been a continuous companion to me during these different stages of my life, changing alongside me and occasionally exposing its secrets in unexpected ways. Route 66 has a special place in my heart, whether it's from the nostalgia of old motels, the friendliness of neighborhood diners, or the amazing views of the surrounding countryside.

I've placed a lot of my experience from all these years into this book to give you a thorough understanding of this iconic road. In addition to the well-known sights and activities, I want to highlight the undiscovered gems that add even more special touches to Route 66. I want to convey to you the many aspects of American culture that make this road so cherished, from the allure of small-town festivals to the history behind historical markers.

So fasten your seatbelts and get ready for a voyage that will take you off the actual road. Let's take a closer look at the colorful towns, varied terrain, and rich history that make up Route 66. Greetings from a unique road trip where each mile narrates a tale and each destination presents a fresh experience.

Toni Myles.

Chapter 2. Planning Your Trip

Best Time to Travel

The timing of your Route 66 trip might greatly improve your experience. This traditional road trip is best taken in the spring (April to June) or fall (September to October). These seasons will make your journey more enjoyable with their nice temperatures and less likelihood of extreme weather. Spring brings with it blossoming landscapes and warm weather, while fall brings with it crisper air and gorgeous fall leaves.

Summer (July to August) can be very hot, with frequent highs above 100°F (38°C), particularly in the desert regions of New Mexico and Arizona. If you intend to travel at this time of year, make sure your car is built to handle long trips in hot weather and be ready for the heat. Summertime also brings in more travelers, which could mean congested hotels and attractions.

Winter has a distinct set of difficulties, spanning from November to March. While there are some nice places, especially in the southern states, there may be snow and ice in the northern and higher elevation regions, which makes driving conditions more dangerous. Winter travel, however, can provide a more sedate experience with fewer visitors and cheaper lodging costs.

A Must-have Packing List

- **Comfortable Clothes:** Bring layers for colder climates and lightweight, breathable clothing for warmer climates. Add a lightweight sweater or jacket for chilly nights and unforeseen temperature fluctuations.
- **Sturdy Footwear**: When touring historical monuments and roadside attractions, comfortable walking shoes are a must. If you intend to go hiking or explore the outdoors, think about bringing hiking shoes.
- **Sun Protection**: To protect oneself from the sun, especially in the more arid parts of the route, carry sunscreen, sunglasses, and a wide-brimmed hat.
- **Maps and Travel Guides**: Although GPS is a useful tool, having a real map and travel guide can improve your trip and offer backup navigation in case it's needed.
- **First Aid box**: Bring bandages, antiseptic wipes, painkillers, and other personal prescriptions you might require in a basic first aid box.
- **Reusable Water Bottle**: It's important to stay hydrated, particularly when driving for extended periods. Reusable water bottles will save waste and help you stay hydrated.
- **Snacks**: To avoid starvation on long drives between towns, carry a variety of snacks in your car. Pack non-perishable goods like granola bars, almonds, and dried fruit.
- **Camera or Smartphone**: Use a camera or smartphone to record the moments from your travels. You'll want to keep in mind the charming scenery and unique attractions along Route 66.

- **Car Essentials**: Make sure your vehicle is properly maintained and include roadside emergency supplies, a spare tire, a jack, and jumper cables.
- **Cash and Cards**: Although credit cards are accepted everywhere, some smaller, historic buildings and restaurants may require cash payments. Having all options at your disposal is a wise move.
- **Travel Insurance**: To cover unforeseen circumstances like trip cancellations, medical emergencies, or car problems, think about getting travel insurance.
- **Pen and Notebook**: You can record travel observations, travel notes, or significant information about the locations you visit in a notebook.

You'll be ready to take advantage of everything that Route 66 has to offer if you plan your vacation keeping these things in mind. A smoother and more pleasurable trip is guaranteed whether you're seeing historical sites, sampling regional food, or finding hidden treasures.

Budgeting and Costs

It's possible to have an amazing and fulfilling experience when traveling Route 66, but making the most of your trip without going over budget requires careful planning. Here is a sample budget plan to get you started, along with a guide to help you plan your budget.

Costs of Lodging

The location, kind of stay, and time of year all affect how much accommodation along Route 66 costs. You may find a variety of accommodations, from boutique hotels and historic lodges to inexpensive motels and roadside inns. Generally speaking:

- **Budget Motels/Inns:** $60 - $100 per night
- **Mid-Range Hotels:** $100 - $150 per night
- **Boutique Hotels/Unique Stays:** $150 - $250+ per night

Dining Costs

Local eateries, fast food chains, and vintage diners can all be found along Route 66. By your preferences, set aside money:

- **Budget Meals (Fast Food/Diners):** $10 - $20 per meal
- **Mid-Range Restaurants:** $20 - $40 per meal
- **Specialty Dining:** $40 - $60+ per meal

Fuel Prices

The fuel economy of your car and the price of gas at the time will determine how much fuel you use. Gas might cost anything from $3 to $5 per gallon on average. You can calculate the following for a round-trip distance along Route 66, which is roughly 2,448 miles:

- **Average Fuel Efficiency:** 25 miles per gallon
- **Total Gallons Needed:** Approximately 98 gallons
- **Estimated Fuel Cost:** $300 - $500 (depending on gas prices)

Attraction Fees

Numerous museums and roadside attractions along Route 66 have little or no free admission. Nonetheless, certain well-known locations could charge more for admission:

- **Typical Attraction Fees:** $5 - $20 per person
- **Special Tours or Experiences:** $20 - $50+ per person

Miscellaneous

- **Souvenirs:** $10 - $50 (varies based on personal preferences)
- **Parking Fees:** $5 - $15 per day (if applicable)
- **Unexpected Costs:** $50 - $100 (emergency funds or additional expenses)

Sample Budget Plan

Here's a sample budget plan for a 10-day Route 66 trip, assuming moderate spending:

- **Accommodation (10 nights):**
  - Budget Motels: $80 per night x 10 nights = $800
- **Dining (3 meals per day):**
  - Average of $30 per day x 10 days = $300
- **Fuel:**
  - Estimated at $400 for the round trip
- **Attractions and Activities:**
  - Average of $15 per person x 10 attractions = $150
- **Miscellaneous Expenses:**
  - Souvenirs: $50
  - Parking Fees: $10 per day x 10 days = $100

- Unexpected Costs: $75

Total Estimated Budget:

- Accommodation: $800
- Dining: $300
- Fuel: $400
- Attractions: $150
- Miscellaneous: $225

Total: $1,875

This budget plan provides a general estimate to help you plan your Route 66 adventure. Adjust the figures based on your preferences, travel style, and specific plans. By planning your budget carefully, you can ensure a stress-free and enjoyable journey along this historic and iconic road.

Chapter 3. Route 66 Overview

The Route's History and Evolution

Known by many as the "Main Street of America," Route 66 was created on November 11, 1926, as one of the first U.S. roads. It was intended to link the sunny beaches of the West Coast with the busy industrial centers of the Midwest, stretching 2,448 miles from Chicago, Illinois, to Santa Monica, California. With its establishment, the American highway system underwent a dramatic change and passengers now had a more direct path throughout the nation.

- **Early Life and Importance**

Route 66 was first a disorganized network of pre-existing roads and highways. Its course changed throughout time as sections were paved and upgraded, reflecting the quick developments in infrastructure and vehicle technology in the early 20th century. It soon established itself as a crucial route for trade and travel, making it easier for people and products to move around the nation.

Because it served as a lifeline for thousands of Dust Bowl-affected families moving west in pursuit of better opportunities, Route 66 earned the moniker "Mother Road" during the Great Depression. The highway was a symbol of resilience and optimism, and The Grapes of Wrath by John Steinbeck memorialized its connection to these "Okies" and other migrants.

- **Mid-Century Elegance**

Route 66 reached its heyday in the middle of the 20th century. As the public in America gained greater access to automobiles, the highway thrived as a top destination for road trips. The route was lined with roadside attractions, hotels, and neon-lit diners, making it the epitome of an American road trip. During this time, road trips were increasingly popular and the car culture emerged, making Route 66 a byword for adventure and freedom.

- **Obstacles and Decline**

Route 66 had difficulties as the Interstate Highway System grew in the 1950s and 1960s. There has been a decrease in traffic on Route 66 due to the construction of Interstate 40, which runs almost exactly parallel to it. This was made possible by faster and more efficient travel. Officially, Route 66 was discontinued as a U.S. highway in 1985. highway, which was supplanted by contemporary interstates and avoided many of the once-thriving small towns and tourist destinations along the route.

- **Restoration and Conservation**

Route 66 has seen a rise in interest and preservation efforts despite being decommissioned. A significant effort to honor and promote the historic route emerged in the 1990s. The distinct character of Route 66 has been preserved, historical tourism has been promoted, and landmarks have been restored and maintained by a variety of groups, local communities, and preservationists.

As a cultural icon and a representation of the American road trip tradition, Route 66 is honored today. Travelers from all over the world come here to take in its historical significance and nostalgic appeal. The route provides a trip through

American history, highlighting the development of the nation's roadside architecture, small communities, and automotive culture.

- **History and Significance**

The influence of Route 66 goes beyond its actual path. It has impacted pop culture in the United States, encompassing music, movies, and literature. Memorabilia, music, and endless stories honoring the highway's illustrious past represent its legacy. The route embodies the essence of the American road trip and is a monument to the persistent spirit of adventure and discovery.

In conclusion, Route 66 is a historic trip through the American experience rather than merely a route. Its transformation from an essential trade route to a cherished cultural icon illustrates both its historical relevance in the formation of the country and its enduring appeal as a symbol of freedom and adventure.

Key Landmarks and Attractions

These sites and landmarks are just a few of the many experiences that Route 66 has to offer. Every location along the way contributes a distinct chapter to the tale of America's cherished highway, weaving a rich fabric of culture, history, and adventure.

Chicago, Illinois – The Starting Point

The formal beginning point of Route 66 is Chicago, the busy city on the shores of Lake Michigan. Chicago provides a plethora of exciting sites and activities to get your road trip off to a great start.

Costs and What to Expect :

- **Accommodations**: There are many different lodging alternatives in Chicago, ranging from deluxe stays to affordable hotels. A mid-range hotel will cost you between $100 and $250 per night on average. The Chicago Athletic Association Hotel and Palmer House Hilton are well-liked options close to downtown.
- **Dining**: The price of dining varies a lot. For $15 to $25 per person, you can have dinner at a simple diner, or you can spend $50 or more on a fancy dining experience.
- **Attractions**: Adult entry to major sights such as the Art Institute of Chicago costs about $25. The Willis Tower Skydeck, which provides breathtaking city views, charges between $30 and $40.

Routes and Driving Information:

- **Starting Point**: Situated in the center of downtown Chicago, at the intersection of Adams Street and Michigan Avenue, is the official Route 66 Begin Sign.
- **Route Details**: Route 66 leaves Chicago and travels southwest across Illinois, passing through a mixture of rural and urban areas. You will travel through charming villages and picturesque roads on the first part of your journey, which will prepare you for the variety of experiences that lie ahead.
- **What to Expect**: Chicago's vibrant blend of history, culture, and contemporary attractions will remain available in 2024 and 2025. Anticipate a dynamic metropolis including a thriving arts scene, recognizable architecture, and lively neighborhoods.

Be ready for heavy traffic, especially during rush hours. To get around the city's congested streets, think about taking public transit or utilizing ridesharing services.

Joliet, Illinois – Historic Sites

Joliet, a fascinating look into the history of Route 66, is only a short journey southwest of Chicago. This city is a memorable stop on your travels because of its distinctive attractions and historic sites.

Costs and What to Expect:

- **Accommodations**: Compared to Chicago, Joliet offers generally more reasonably priced lodging options. For low-cost motels, expect to pay between $60 and $100 per night, and for mid-range hotels, between $100 and $150. With extra conveniences, the Harrah's Joliet Casino Hotel provides a comfortable stay.
- **Dining**: Meals at neighborhood diners or informal restaurants run between $10 and $20 per person, making Joliet a reasonably affordable dining destination.

Routes and Driving Information:

- **Driving Directions**: Take Interstate 55 South to Joliet from Chicago. Depending on the amount of traffic, the roughly 40-mile travel usually takes 45 minutes.
- **Route Information**: You'll notice a change in scenery as you journey from Chicago's urban setting to Joliet's more suburban and historic neighborhoods.

This section of Route 66 is signposted and takes you by several historical landmarks in the area.

What to Expect: With well-preserved historical attractions and a friendly ambiance, Joliet will continue to embrace its Route 66 heritage from 2024–2025. Important attractions include:

- **Joliet Route 66 Museum**: Housed inside the Joliet Area Historical Museum, this museum provides a thorough examination of the history and culture of Route 66 through interactive exhibits, vintage signage, and memorabilia.
- **Joliet Prison**: Though it is no longer in use, guided tours of the prison offer an intriguing look into its history as a maximum-security establishment. The tours reflect the prison's illustrious past and are both educational and occasionally spooky.

All things considered, Joliet is a noteworthy destination on your route because of its historic attractiveness and proximity to Route 66. As you go on your journey down this fabled roadway, anticipate a mix of historical exploration and warm local hospitality.

St. Louis, Missouri – Iconic Landmarks

Route 66 passes through the dynamic city of St. Louis, which is well-known for its historical significance and cultural landmarks. There are many sights to see as you drive through this well-known city that showcases its fascinating past as well as its contemporary beauty.

Costs and What to Expect:

- **Accommodations**: There are a range of affordable hotel alternatives in St. Louis. Mid-range hotels should cost between $90 and $180 per night on average. Both the Drury Plaza Hotel St. Louis at the Arch and the Hyatt Regency St. Louis at the Arch are well-liked options for cozy stays near major attractions.
- **Dining**: There are a variety of affordable and high-end dining alternatives in St. Louis. While luxury dining can cost anywhere from $50 to $80 or more per person, a casual lunch will likely cost between $15 and $30 per person.
- **Attractions**: A good number of the main attractions in St. Louis are affordable. For example, the $40 adult cost of the tram ride includes admission to the Gateway Arch's museum. A family favorite, the St. Louis Zoo admits free of charge.

Routes and Driving Information:

- **Driving Directions**: Take Interstate 55 South to reach St. Louis from Joliet. Depending on traffic and stops along the route, the approximately 300-mile travel usually takes 5 to 6 hours.
- **Route Information**: Well-marked Route 66 leads you through the city's historic districts and toward its main sights as soon as you enter St. Louis. Both the city's busy core and its more laid-back suburban sections are simple to travel thanks to the well-planned route system.

What to Expect: St. Louis will still provide a unique combination of modern and historical experiences in 2024 and 2025. Anticipate a city with a rich cultural legacy, as seen by its well-known sites and energetic neighborhoods. St. Louis's showpiece, the Gateway Arch, continues to provide both breathtaking views and historical insight. Be ready for city traffic, particularly in the vicinity of well-known tourist attractions. For convenience, think about taking public transit or ridesharing.

Springfield, Missouri – Route 66 Heritage

The third-biggest city in Missouri, Springfield, is well known for its historical significance and close ties to Route 66. It offers a sentimental trip through this famous highway's past.

Costs and What to Expect:

- **Accommodations**: Springfield has a variety of hotel choices, with mid-range hotels usually costing between $70 and $120 per night. Notable options include the Hilton Garden Inn Springfield and the University Plaza Hotel.
- **Dining**: There are reasonably priced informal dining alternatives in Springfield, with prices per person ranging from $12 to $25. The well-known Route 66 Diner, renowned for its nostalgic atmosphere and substantial dishes, is a local favorite.

Routes and Driving Information:

- **Driving Route**: Traveling from St. Louis to Springfield entails travel of around 100 miles via Interstate 44 West, which normally takes around 1.5 to 2 hours.
- **Route Details**: Traveling along this section of Route 66, you'll pass through charming small towns and picturesque rural settings. Springfield's main

attractions are easily accessible thanks to the city's layout and well-marked Route 66 sites.

What to Expect: Springfield will honor its Route 66 history in 2024–2025 by adding several noteworthy attractions.

- **Route 66 Car Museum**: This museum offers a nostalgic journey back in time with its vast collection of vintage vehicles and souvenirs from the Route 66 era.
- **The Original Steak 'n Shake:** The Original Steak 'n Shake is a legendary Route 66 restaurant known for its shakes and burgers as well as its significance to the development of roadside dining in the United States.
- **The Springfield Route 66 Visitor Center:** The Springfield Route 66 Visitor Center is conveniently located in the city's downtown and offers maps, pamphlets, and useful information about the city's Route 66 attractions.

Springfield's dedication to preserving Route 66 history assures that visitors may have an authentic and enriching experience. Anticipate a warm environment with many chances to discover the rich history of this famous road, including vintage auto museums and diners.

Tulsa, Oklahoma – Cultural Hotspot

The dynamic city of Tulsa, Oklahoma, provides a wide range of historical, cultural, and artistic activities. Discovering Tulsa will reveal that it is a major stop on the Route 66 route, offering a glimpse of its present cultural scene as well as its historic appeal.

Costs and What to Expect:

22

- **Accommodation**: There are several places to stay in Tulsa; mid-range hotels often go between $80 and $130 a night. For cozy lodging, think about booking a room at the Hyatt Regency Tulsa or the Ambassador Hotel Tulsa.
- **Dining**: There are many different places to eat in Tulsa, and informal eateries often charge between $10 and $25 per person. Visit The Tavern for a distinctive dining experience; it's well-known for its inventive menu and vibrant ambiance.

Routes and Driving Information:

- **Driving Directions**: Take Interstate 44 West to get from Springfield to Tulsa. The trip takes four to five hours on average, covering a distance of about 300 miles.
- **Route Details**: Travel through Oklahoma's tiny towns and undulating plains on this section of Route 66. The well-marked Route 66 landmarks in Tulsa are a testament to the city's rich history and cultural establishments.

What to Expect: Tulsa will be a popular destination for culture in 2025, offering a variety of attractions.

- **Tulsa's Route 66 Historic District:** The Route 66 Historic District in Tulsa is home to vintage motels, retro diners, and restored neon signs that perfectly encapsulate the spirit of the historic route. You can roam about and take in the atmosphere of the past here.
- **Philbrook Museum of Art**: Set in a magnificent Italian-style estate, this museum is a must-see for art

lovers with an amazing collection of artwork and wonderfully designed grounds.
- **The Tulsa Arts District:** The Tulsa Arts District is a bustling neighborhood that reflects the city's burgeoning arts sector with its many galleries, performing venues, and unique businesses.

Tulsa offers a rich and interesting stop on your Route 66 journey with its blend of historical and cultural attractions. You can anticipate a city that is both deeply rooted in its history and has a thriving modern cultural scene, making for an unforgettable and engaging vacation experience.

Amarillo, Texas – Quirky Attractions

The vibrant Texas Panhandle city of Amarillo provides a distinctive blend of oddball sights and vintage Route 66 adventures. There are many unique and entertaining places to see in Amarillo that encapsulate the essence of this famous route.

Costs and What to Expect:

- **Accommodation:** There are several lodging alternatives in Amarillo, with mid-range motels usually charging between $70 and $120 per night. The Courtyard by Marriott Amarillo and the Drury Inn & Suites Amarillo are well-liked options.
- **Dining:** There are a variety of informal and interesting dining options in Amarillo. In casual dining establishments such as neighborhood dinners, budget approximately $10 to $25 per person. Try the Big Texan Steak Ranch—famous for its 72-ounce steak challenge—for an unforgettable dining experience.

- **Attractions**: A lot of Amarillo's unusual sights can be seen for free or for a small price. For instance, entrance to the American Quarter Horse Hall of Fame & Museum costs approximately $10, yet the Cadillac Ranch is an outdoor art piece that is free to view.

Routes and Driving Information:

- **Driving Directions**: Take Interstate 40 East to get to Amarillo from Albuquerque. The trip is roughly 290 miles long and often takes four to five hours.
- **Route Information**: Route 66 leads you through the Texas Panhandle's level terrain as you head east, with Amarillo providing a vibrant mix of roadside attractions and traditional Route 66 charm.

What to Expect: Amarillo will keep showcasing its unique and eccentric attractions in 2025. Important pauses include:

- **Cadillac Ranch** is a well-known public art piece that consists of ten old Cadillacs that have been graffitied and buried nose-down in a field. Because of its distinctive artistic expression and engaging experience, it's a must-see.
- **Big Texan Steak Ranch:** Well-known for its famous steak challenge, this eatery is also a lot of fun for a filling lunch because of its vibrant décor and Old West ambiance.
- **American Quarter Horse Hall of Fame & Museum:** With displays on the breed's significance in American culture, this museum honors the history and legacy of the American Quarter Horse.

Amarillo is a unique destination on your trip because of its unique attractions and legacy as a Route 66 city. Anticipate a dynamic metropolis with a distinct personality and plenty of chances for unforgettable encounters and photo opportunities.

Albuquerque, New Mexico – Cultural Richness

A thorough exploration of the history and culture of Route 66 may be found in Albuquerque, a city known for its thriving arts scene and rich cultural legacy. You'll find a variety of attractions that showcase the city's varied influences as you explore Albuquerque.

Costs and What to Expect:

- **Accommodation**: Albuquerque offers a choice of accommodations, with mid-range hotels ranging in price from $80 to $140 a night. Popular options that provide comfort and convenience are the Albuquerque Marriott and the Hotel Albuquerque at Old Town.
- **Dining** in Albuquerque can be both inexpensive and fancy. Aim for $15 to $30 per person when dining at nearby establishments. Try El Pinto for a taste of the local flavor; it's well-known for its authentic New Mexican food.
- **Accomodation**: A lot of Albuquerque's cultural sites have inexpensive admission costs. For instance, entry to the Indian Pueblo Cultural Center is about $8, whereas the Albuquerque Museum is about $10.

Routes and Driving Information:

- **Driving Directions**: Take Interstate 40 West to get from Amarillo to Albuquerque. The trip usually takes four to five hours, covering a distance of about 290 miles.
- **Route Information**: Route 66 leads you into the center of Albuquerque, which is home to a variety of historical and cultural sites, after passing through picturesque desert landscapes as you head west.

What to Expect: Albuquerque will still provide a diverse range of cultural events in 2025.

- **Old Town Albuquerque** is a historic area that offers a window into the Spanish colonial past of the city with its adobe structures, galleries, and stores. It's a wonderful location to sample authentic New Mexican cuisine and local crafts.
- The **Albuquerque Museum is** housed in Old Town and features displays of local history, art, and culture that shed light on the rich diversity of the city's past.
- **Indian Pueblo Cultural Center**: This center features performances and displays that highlight the customs and contributions of the Pueblo people, showcasing their art, history, and culture.

Route 66 travelers should not miss Albuquerque, which has a thriving cultural scene and interesting historical sites. Anticipate a city that offers a variety of contemporary conveniences and cultural pleasures, all while celebrating its rich history.

Kingman, Arizona – Route 66 Hub

A major hub on Route 66, Kingman, Arizona, is renowned for its rich local culture and historical significance. A multitude of attractions honoring the Mother Road's legacy may be found around Kingman.

Costs and What to Expect:

- **Accommodations**: There are several places to stay in Kingman, with mid-range motels usually charging between $70 and $110 a night. Two well-liked options are the Holiday Inn Express Kingman and the Best Western Plus Kingman.
- **Dining**: Meals at neighborhood diners and informal eateries run between $10 and $20 per person, making dining alternatives in Kingman reasonably priced. The Route 66 Grill serves food with a Route 66 motif.
- **Attractions**: A lot of the attractions along Route 66 in Kingman are either free or charge a nominal admission fee. It costs about $5 to enter the Kingman Route 66 Museum, however it is free to enter the Powerhouse Visitor Center.

Routes and Driving Information:

- **Driving Directions**: Take Interstate 40 West to get to Kingman from Albuquerque. The trip usually takes five to six hours, covering a distance of around 340 miles.
- **Route details**: Travelers on this section of Route 66 pass through the untamed regions of northern Arizona, and Kingman is an important destination for fans of the historic route.

What to Expect: Kingman will remain a major hub for Route 66 exploration in 2025.

- **The Kingman Route 66 Museum** is housed at the Powerhouse Visitor Center and has a large collection of antique signs, pictures, and historical relics, among other Route 66 memorabilia.
- **Route 66 Historic District**: Take a tour of the town's conserved historic structures and murals, which pay homage to Route 66's legacy and provide a nostalgic window into the past.
- **Mohave Museum of History & Arts**: This museum offers more background information on the history of the area and the effects of Route 66.

Being a hub for Route 66, Kingman guarantees that tourists may fully immerse themselves in the history and culture of this famous route. Anticipate a friendly community that takes great pride in its Route 66 history and a variety of attractions that emphasize its importance along the Mother Road.

Oatman, Arizona – Ghost Town Charm

A nostalgic window into the past may be found in Oatman, Arizona, a charming ghost town tucked away along a winding section of Route 66. Renowned for its eccentric ambiance, ancient buildings, and amiable burros, Oatman embodies the essence of Route 66 and is a must-visit destination.

Costs and What to Expect:

- **Accommodations:** Kingman, which is close by, has lodging alternatives; Oatman does not have any typical lodging options. In Kingman, mid-range hotels typically cost between $70 and $110 a night. Consider

staying in one of the neighboring tiny towns or RV sites if you're looking for a unique experience.
- **Dining**: Oatman has a small yet lovely dining scene. Basic meals are available at the neighborhood café for between $10 and $20 per person. The rustic ambiance offers a taste of traditional Route 66 travel.
- **Attractions**: Many of Oatman's attractions are free, making travel there comparatively inexpensive. Highlights that are free of charge are the historic charm and burro encounters.

Routes and Driving Information:

- **Driving Directions**: Take Route 66 East to Oatman from Kingman. With beautiful views and desert scenery along the route, the 45-minute trip is about 30 miles long.
- **Route information**: The road gets a little rougher and twistier as you get closer to Oatman. The town is a remarkable diversion from the main Route 66 route because of its distinct beauty and historic architecture.

What to Expect: Oatman's cozy environment and ghost town charm will keep drawing tourists in 2024 and 2025.

- **Historic Buildings**: Take a look at the ruins of former shops and structures that encapsulate a bygone period. Offering a window into its past as a thriving center for gold mining, the historic mining town has managed to retain its charm.
- **Burro Encounters**: Oatman's population of wild burros, which wander the town freely, is one of its most notable aspects. These amiable creatures, who

are used to tourists, offer a special touch to the town's allure.
- **Quirky Stores & Artifacts**: Peruse the neighborhood stores' collections of antiques, old photos, and artifacts related to Route 66. The town's unique and colorful atmosphere is ideal for exploring and capturing treasured memories.

Oatman's Route 66 history combined with its ghost town charm makes it a one-of-a-kind destination that takes you back in time. Anticipate a laid-back, historic small-town vibe with lots of chances to soak in the Mother Road spirit.

Santa Monica, California – The End of the Road

The Mother Road comes to an appropriate finale at Santa Monica, California, the famous terminus of Route 66. Concluding this iconic highway, Santa Monica, which is situated on the Pacific coast, offers a combination of breathtaking scenery, a lively cultural scene, and a joyous atmosphere.

Costs and What to Expect:

- **Accommodations**: Santa Monica offers a variety of places to stay, ranging from opulent resorts to low-cost hotels. Budget between $150 and $300 per night for mid-range to expensive lodging. The Shore Hotel and the Hotel Casa del Mar are well-liked options.
- **Dining**: There are many different places to eat in Santa Monica, with meals costing between $20 and $50 per person. Savor a variety of dishes at beloved neighborhood eateries including True Food Kitchen and The Misfit Restaurant + Bar.

- **Attractions**: A wide range of attractions are available at different prices. For instance, while Pacific Park on the Pier may have minimal admission fees for rides and activities, the Santa Monica Pier and beach are free.

Routes and Driving Information:

- **Travel Route**: From Kingman, drive Interstate 40 West to Interstate 15 South, then join onto Interstate 10 West to get to Santa Monica. Depending on traffic, the 400-mile journey takes between 6 and 7 hours to complete.
- **Route Details**: You will go through a variety of environments on this route, including the bustling urban setting of Los Angeles and desert countryside. The energetic city of Santa Monica offers the ideal cap for your Route 66 journey.

What to Expect: Santa Monica will still be a vibrant and scenic way to end your Route 66 adventure in 2025.

- **Santa Monica Pier** is a famous landmark that offers a variety of dining options, an aquarium, and an amusement park. The Ferris wheel at the Pier is a fantastic place to celebrate reaching your destination because it provides breathtaking views of the Pacific Ocean.
- **Santa Monica Beach**: Take in the gorgeous vistas of the Pacific Ocean and the sandy beaches. The beach is a great place to unwind, promenade, or just enjoy the last moments of your Route 66 journey.
- Discover the **Third Street Promenade**, a bustling pedestrian area with eateries, boutiques, and street

performers. It's a terrific spot to take in the local flavor and shop for souvenirs.

Santa Monica offers a colorful and picturesque way to end your journey along Route 66. A celebration of reaching the end of this renowned roadway awaits you, along with a mix of urban excitement and coastal calm.

Chapter 4. Regional Highlights

Illinois

Chicago to St. Louis: Must-See Stops

Route 66 attractions, quaint small villages, and historical places abound along the route that connects Chicago and St. Louis. This section of the road gives visitors a variety of experiences by combining urban energy with picturesque Americana.

Joliet, Illinois

Joliet, a historic city on Route 66, is only a short drive southwest of Chicago. Notable sites along the route include:

- **Joliet Route 66 Museum:** Housed within the Joliet Area Historical Museum, this museum features a variety of antique items, old photographs, and interactive displays to honor the history and culture of Route 66.
- **Joliet Prison**: An important site that provides guided tours exploring the prison's past and architecture, providing guests with a rare look into its days as a maximum-security establishment.

Wilmington, Illinois

Wilmington, which is located further southwest, offers a taste of traditional Route 66 Americana:

- **Route 66 Museum:** This museum, which is housed in the old Rialto Theater, has displays about the history of Route 66 and how it influenced American culture.
- **The Gemini Giant** is a famous roadside landmark that is a must-see Route 66 photo opportunity. It is a massive astronaut statue that stands proudly at the Launching Pad Drive-In.

Braidwood, Illinois

A snapshot of the iconic Route 66 experience can be found at Braidwood:

- **The Old Route 66:** Original diners and hotels that evoke the nostalgia of the Route 66 period help the town maintain its vintage appeal. It's a charming stop because of the vintage vibe of the roadside.

Dwight, Illinois

Dwight is well-known for its vintage Route 66 landmarks:

- The Route 66 relics and memorabilia on display at the Dwight Historical Society Museum provide insights into the significance of the highway and the local history.
- The Ambler-Becker Texaco Station is a historic Route 66 service station that offers a window into the past. It has been rebuilt to resemble what it did in the 1930s.

Pontiac, Illinois

The history and culture of Route 66 are abundant in Pontiac:

- **Route 66 Hall of Fame & Museum:** This museum honors the history of the roadway with a collection of antique signage, relics, and memorabilia. It is situated in Pontiac's downtown.
- **Pontiac's Murals:** The town is recognized for its colorful murals representing Route 66 scenery and historical events, bringing a bright and artistic touch to your visit.

Bloomington, Illinois

There are historical and cultural attractions in Bloomington.

- **The David Davis Mansion** is a superbly maintained Victorian mansion that offers insight into the lives of well-known judge and statesman David Davis from the 19th century.
- Discover the **Historic Downtown Bloomington**, which is home to quaint stores, cafes, and historic buildings.

Lincoln, Illinois

Lincoln is renowned for its legacy along Route 66 and historical significance:

- **Lincoln's Home and Museum:** Abraham Lincoln's former residence is now a museum with guided tours and displays on the life and career of the sixteenth president.
- **The Dixie Truckers Home** is a vintage truck stop and restaurant located on Route 66 that serves hearty meals in a nostalgic setting.

Springfield, Illinois

The state capital of Springfield is a must-see because of its extensive historical and cultural offerings:

- **Abraham Lincoln Presidential Library and Museum**: A wealth of information about Lincoln's life, presidency, and the Civil War era is available at this museum.
- **Lincoln's Tomb**: The last resting place of Abraham Lincoln and his family, it is situated in Oak Ridge Cemetery.

Edwardsville Illinois

Edwardsville, just outside of St. Louis, is a delightful stop:

- Visit the **Edwardsville Historical Museum** to learn about the history of the area and the significance of this Route 66 community.

St. Louis, Missouri

This section of Route 66 ends when you reach St. Louis:

- **The Gateway Arch**, a famous landmark that represents westward migration, offers breathtaking city views from its observation deck.
- The lively neighborhood of **The Delmar Loop** is well-known for its unique selection of eateries, retail establishments, and entertainment options.

Driving Routes and What to Expect:

- **Route Information**: Depending on traffic and the number of stops made, the roughly 300-mile trip from Chicago to St. Louis usually takes five to six hours.
- **Historical and Scenic insights**: This section of Route 66 is home to a variety of urban settings, old-fashioned little towns, and picturesque byways. A mix of nostalgia and contemporary will greet you as you pass through several locales that evoke the rich history of Route 66.

This trip through Illinois provides a fascinating overview of Route 66, including a variety of historical sights, famous landmarks, and traditional roadside attractions found throughout America. Every location offers a different perspective on the past and culture of this fabled route.

Missouri

St. Louis to Springfield: Must-See Stops

Traveling Route 66 from St. Louis to Springfield is a trip filled with breathtaking scenery, fascinating history, and quintessential Americana. This section of Route 66 in Missouri has a lot to offer visitors, from unusual roadside stops to famous urban sites, making it the ideal combination of nostalgia and adventure.

St. Louis, Missouri

The starting point of your Route 66 adventure through Missouri is St. Louis, which offers famous sites and diverse cultural experiences.

- The imposing **Gateway Arch** is a representation of the westward movement. A ride to the summit offers visitors sweeping views of the Mississippi River and the city.
- **Chain of Rocks Bridge**: A distinctive Route 66 landmark with a well-known 30-degree bend, this bridge is now a pedestrian walkway with stunning river views.

Cuba, Missouri

Known as "Mural City," Cuba provides an insight into the history of Route 66 and small-town life.

- **Wagon Wheel Motel**: One of the oldest motels on Route 66 still in operation, this tastefully renovated historic location is a must-visit for anybody seeking a throwback experience.
- **Cuba Murals**: The town is home to several murals that illustrate historical events, Route 66, and folklore from the area. Cuba is a fun place to take pictures because of the colorful artwork that lines the streets.

Rolla, Missouri

Rolla is a college town with stunning scenery and a long history connected to Route 66:

- **Stonehenge Replica**: This half-sized recreation of the well-known English monument is situated on the Missouri S&T campus and is an interesting yet striking visit.
- **Totem Pole Trading Post**: Offering a piece of history along with souvenirs, this trading post is one of the oldest Route 66 establishments still in operation.

Devil's Elbow, Missouri

Tucked down beside the Big Piney River, Devil's Elbow is a charming historical site:

- **Devil's Elbow Bridge**: Located on Route 66, this 1920s steel truss bridge offers breathtaking views of the river below.

- **Elbow Inn Bar & BBQ Pit**: A roadside dive with a fascinating history, this local hangout offers a sense of real Route 66 culture along with delicious barbecue and refreshing cocktails.

Lebanon, Missouri

Lebanon has a unique blend of Missouri warmth and vintage Route 66 charm:

- **Route 66 Museum and Research Center:** This museum, which is housed in the Lebanon-Laclede County Library, has interesting exhibits of antiques and memorabilia from the heyday of Route 66.
- **Munger Moss Motel**: Opened in 1946, the Munger Moss is a well-known retro motel that still sports its original neon sign.

Springfield, Missouri

Springfield, dubbed the "Birthplace of Route 66," honors the essence of the Mother Road:

- **Route 66 Car Museum**: Visitors can take a nostalgic trip through automotive history at this museum, which is home to an amazing collection of historic vehicles and Route 66 artifacts.
- **Gillioz Theatre**: Located in Springfield's downtown, this historic theater still performs acts and provides a window into the city's architecture from the 1920s.

Driving Routes and What to Expect:

- **Route Information**: Depending on how many stops you make along the way, the 215-mile drive from St. Louis to Springfield should take you 3 to 4 hours.
- **Historical and Scenic Insights**: You can anticipate a tour with undulating hills, luxuriant vegetation, and charming villages. The Missouri section of Route 66 is well-known for its picturesque scenery, welcoming residents, and intense nostalgia for the Mother Road's glory days.

For any traveler, this section of Missouri's Route 66 offers a captivating and unforgettable experience by showcasing both rural beauty and urban excitement.

Kansas

Springfield to the Oklahoma Border: Unique Sites

Even though there are just 13 miles of Route 66 in Kansas, that little distance is rich in beauty and history. There are several distinctive locations and attractions along the Mother Road that encapsulate its essence, spanning from Springfield to the border with Oklahoma.

Galena, Kansas

The first town you'll come across in Kansas is called Galena, and it offers a welcoming and historic atmosphere.

- **Cars on the Route:** This renovated Kan-O-Tex gas station is well-known for its association with the animated film Cars. This eccentric location offers picture opportunities with "Tow Mater" and other vehicle-themed attractions.
- Explore the rich mining history of the area at the **Galena Mining & Historical Museum**, which has displays and artifacts from the town's former lead and zinc mining days.

Riverton, Kansas

One of the most famous locations on Route 66 is at Riverton:

- **Old Riverton shop (Eisler Brothers):** Still a Route 66 staple, this vintage general shop has been in operation since 1925. With an interior that transports you to the heyday of the road, it's a terrific spot to grab food and souvenirs.
- One of the last surviving marsh arch bridges on Route 66, **Rainbow Bridge** was built in 1923 and is a must-see photo stop for anyone who enjoys taking road trips.

Baxter Springs, Kansas

Known as the "First Cowtown in Kansas," Baxter Springs offers a unique fusion of Route 66 culture and history.

- The **Baxter Springs Heritage Center & Museum** provides a thorough examination of the history of the area, including everything from its Native American origins to its involvement in the Civil War and the creation of Route 66.

- Situated in the storied Crowell Bank Building, **Cafe on the Route** provides a flavor of traditional Route 66 cuisine. The structure itself has a notorious past because Jesse James once robbed it.

Driving Routes and What to Expect:

- **Route Information**: Although the Kansas portion of Route 66 is only 13 miles long, it is jam-packed with attractions. It will take roughly 20 minutes to travel across Kansas, but give yourself more time to stop and enjoy the tiny villages along the way.

- **Views from the Scenic and Historical** Side: Anticipate a laid-back and enchanting trip through little communities that have kept Route 66 landmarks. The people who live along the Kansas stretch of Route 66 are deeply committed to preserving its history, and the area is rich in Americana.

Despite being short, the Kansas portion of Route 66 is chock full of interesting locations that capture the essence of the open road. On this famous highway, it's the ideal illustration of how small-town America can provide unforgettable experiences.

Oklahoma

The Heart of Route 66: Iconic Stops

With more than 400 miles of Route 66, Oklahoma has the longest stretch of any state. If you want to see the real spirit of Route 66, you have to visit Oklahoma, a state well-known for its small communities, historical landmarks, and scenic drives. This section has something for everyone, from interesting roadside stops to important cultural sites.

Tulsa, Oklahoma

Tulsa, a dynamic city, combines the charm of the modern metropolis with the nostalgia of Route 66:

- **Route 66 Rising**: This beautiful steel sculpture in Cyrus Avery Centennial Plaza celebrates Tulsa's significance as the birthplace of Route 66, symbolizing its enduring heritage.
- The famed Route 66 landmark, the **Meadow Gold Sign**, is a restored neon sign dating back to the 1930s and makes for a fantastic photo op.
- **Blue Dome District**: A bustling hub of entertainment in downtown Tulsa, the Blue Dome District offers a blend of contemporary fun and heritage with its array of eateries, retail establishments, and live music venues.

Sapulpa, Oklahoma

Sapulpa has both contemporary and historical Route 66 attractions:

- The **Waite Phillips Filling Station Museum** provides an insight into the history of Route 66 and the Phillips family, who were instrumental in the growth of the region. The museum has been renovated from a gas station.
- The **Heart of Route 66 Auto Museum** is a must-visit location for auto aficionados. It features vintage vehicles and souvenirs related to Route 66, providing a nostalgic look back at the heyday of the Mother Road.

Arcadia, Oklahoma

Arcadia is a little town with a lot to offer, including one of the most famous monuments on Route 66:

- Constructed in 1898, **The Round Barn** is a prime example of pioneering engineering and is now a well-liked destination for visitors traveling along Route 66. Inside, there is a museum, a gift store, and an event space.
- **Pops 66 Soda Ranch** is a contemporary, fun attraction with over 700 different soda flavors from around the globe and a striking 66-foot-tall soda bottle that is lit up with neon lights at night.

Chandler, Oklahoma

Chandler is a quaint, historic hamlet located along Route 66.

- The **Route 66 Interpretive Center** is a museum including films and interactive displays that chronicle the history of Route 66 and its influence on the American experience. It is housed in a former arsenal.
- **McJerry's Route 66 Gallery**: This one-of-a-kind gallery showcases pieces by artist Jerry McClanahan, whose creations have come to represent the road's cultural comeback. The artwork is inspired by Route 66.

Stroud, Oklahoma

The charming hamlet of Stroud continues to honor the heyday of Route 66:

- **Rock Café**: A 1939 historic restaurant, the Rock Café offers traditional diner meals in a quaint, rustic environment. The café's owner served as an inspiration for Sally Carrera, a character in Pixar's Cars, which is another reason for its fame.

Oklahoma City, Oklahoma

There are many Route 66 landmarks to discover in the state capital, including:

- **The Milk Bottle Building** is a peculiar monument that has been a fixture of Route 66 since the 1930s. It is a small building with a huge milk bottle on its roof.
- **The National Cowboy & Western Heritage Museum** is a fantastic place to stop down on any road trip through Oklahoma, even though it's not just off Route 66. It provides visitors with an in-depth look into the history and culture of the American West.

Clinton, Oklahoma

Known as the "Hub City of Western Oklahoma," Clinton provides travelers traveling Route 66 with a must-visit location:

- **Oklahoma Route 66 Museum**: With displays that include artifacts, photos, and music from the route's heyday, this museum provides visitors with an immersive look into the history of the Mother Road.

Elk City, Oklahoma

Elk City's Route 66 attractions are interesting and instructive.

- The **National Route 66 Museum Complex** is a family-friendly destination where visitors can discover the history of the route thanks to life-size replicas of iconic Route 66 establishments and automobiles.

Driving Routes and What to Expect:

- **Route Information:** Depending on how many stops are made, the approximately 400-mile Oklahoman section of Route 66 may take six to eight hours to complete.
- **Scenic and Historical Insights:** This section highlights the big plains, friendly small towns, and extensive history of Oklahoma. Traveling through the center of Route 66 will offer you a taste of both

modern rejuvenation and classic American atmosphere.

With the ideal blend of vintage eateries, roadside curiosities, and historical sites, this trip across Oklahoma provides travelers with the typical Route 66 experience.

Texas

Amarillo to the New Mexico Border: Noteworthy Attractions

Although Texas's Route 66 is shorter than other states, it more than makes up for its shorter length with eye-catching, eccentric attractions. From Amarillo to the border with New Mexico, there are plenty of roadside peculiarities, expansive vistas, and that distinct Texan charm that make this section of the Mother Road an absolute must-see.

Amarillo, Texas

One of the liveliest cities on Texas Route 66 is Amarillo, which is well-known for its oddball roadside attractions and Western culture.

- One of the most famous sites on Route 66 is **Cadillac Ranch**, where ten vintage Cadillacs are buried headfirst in the earth. Bring your spray paint so you can add your graffiti to the ever-evolving art piece.
- A Texas icon, **The Big Texan Steak Ranch** is a roadside eatery well-known for its 72-ounce steak challenge. The large meals and authentic Old West atmosphere make it worth visiting even if you decide not to take on the challenge.

- **Sixth Street Historic District**: This area of Amarillo is traversed by Route 66, which is lined with vintage diners, unique boutiques, and antique stores that take tourists back to the glory of the road.

Vega, Texas

Vega provides a more sedate and nostalgic experience along Route 66:

- **Dot's Mini Museum**: Vega's history and the surrounding area are chronicled through a delightful assortment of Route 66 relics displayed in Dot's Mini Museum. Anyone interested in learning more about the history and culture of the area should swing by.
- **Magnolia Station**: A famous photo stop for Route 66 aficionados, Magnolia Station is a beautifully preserved petrol station that dates back to the 1920s.

Adrian, Texas

Adrian serves as a metaphorical rest break along Route 66, marking its geographic midpoint:

- **Midpoint Café**: Offering passengers a chance to commemorate this milestone, the Midpoint Café is located precisely halfway between Chicago and Los Angeles. Familiar from its Route 66 days, this café boasts charm and history and is well-known for its "ugly crust" pies.
- **Midpoint Sign**: This sign, which is right outside the café, indicates the precise midpoint of Route 66 and is a favorite location for pictures to capture the memories of your trip down the Mother Road.

Glenrio, Texas/New Mexico Border

Glenrio is a ghost town that seems to have been frozen in time and lies where Texas and New Mexico meet:

- **Ghost Town Remains**: Glenrio was formerly a thriving Route 66 town, but since the interstate passed it, it has largely been abandoned. Old motels, petrol stations, and cafes are still visible to visitors, providing an eerie window into the past of life along Route 66.
- **Welcome to New Mexico Sign:** The iconic Route 66 shield that welcomes you to the Land of Enchantment can be seen as soon as you cross the border into New Mexico. This makes for a great photo opportunity before you drive west.

Driving Routes and What to Expect:

- **Route Details**: Depending on how long you stay at each stop, the 115-mile trip from Amarillo to the New Mexico border usually takes between 1.5 and 2 hours.
- **Historical and Scenic insights**: This section of Route 66 is renowned for its unusual roadside attractions and wide-open, expansive scenery. Along the Mother Road, one may anticipate seeing expansive views, quaint small-town Texas charm, and a proud but disappearing past.

This short but lovely stretch of Route 66 across Texas offers a unique combination of historical sites, creative installations, and breathtaking scenery.

New Mexico

The Land of Enchantment: Key Stops

Route 66 in New Mexico is well-known for its breathtaking desert vistas, rich cultural legacy, and strong ties to Native American and Hispanic customs. A fascinating Route 66 experience is guaranteed as you pass through the Land of Enchantment, which is home to a variety of energetic communities, interesting historical sites, and breathtaking natural formations.

Tucumcari, New Mexico

Known as the "Gateway to New Mexico," Tucumcari offers a plethora of vintage Route 66 attractions.

- The Tucumcari Historical Museum, which is housed in a former schoolhouse, features displays and memorabilia about the history of Tucumcari and its connection to Route 66.
- **Blue Swallow Motel**: Located on Route 66, this iconic motel is well-known for its retro neon sign and rooms that evoke the 1940s. It's among the Mother Road's most recognizable and picturesque locations.
- **Route 66 Monument**: Honoring Tucumcari's long-standing relationship with Route 66, this imposing monument is a well-liked photo opportunity.

Santa Rosa, New Mexico

Santa Rosa has the charm of Route 66 and the beauty of the natural world.

- **Blue Hole:** An unexpected oasis in the middle of the desert, this sapphire-blue, spring-fed swimming hole is a popular destination for swimmers and divers.
- **Route 66 Auto Museum**: This museum is a must-see for lovers of vintage automobiles because it has an amazing collection of antique cars and Route 66 memorabilia.

Albuquerque, New Mexico

The biggest city in New Mexico and a center of culture along Route 66 in Albuquerque:

- Experience the fascinating fusion of Native American, Hispanic, and Anglo cultures in **Old Town Albuquerque**, a historic district brimming with stores, eateries, and museums.
- **El Vado Motel:** One of the best examples of how Route 66 locations are being rejuvenated is this superbly restored motel. The retro-style rooms and vintage neon signs provide the ideal balance of comfort and nostalgia.
- **Albuquerque Museum**: With exhibitions on Native American art, Route 66, and the Southwest, this museum offers a thorough look into the history and culture of Albuquerque.

Laguna Pueblo, New Mexico

A look into the rich Native American heritage of New Mexico can be found in Laguna Pueblo:

- One of the oldest mission churches in the United States, **Laguna Mission Church** was founded in the 1600s and continues to be an important part of

Laguna Pueblo's religious and cultural life. Discover the history and customs of the Pueblo while seeing this stunning historic monument.

Gallup, New Mexico

The heritage of Route 66 and Native American culture are deeply ingrained in Gallup.

- **El Rancho Hotel:** dubbed the "Home of the Movie Stars," El Rancho has played host to several Hollywood stars while Westerns have been filmed in the region. It is a well-liked destination for Route 66 tourists because of its vintage charm and memorabilia.
- **The Gallup Cultural Center** showcases the town's strong ties to Native American art and culture by providing local goods and exhibitions.

Driving Routes and What to Expect:

- **Route Information:** Depending on how many stops you make, traveling 380 miles across New Mexico on Route 66 may take six to seven hours.
- **Historical and Scenic Insights**: As you go along New Mexico's Route 66, you can anticipate seeing breathtaking desert vistas, soaring mesas, and energetic cities brimming with culture.

Discovering New Mexico's Route 66 offers visitors an unforgettable trip through the center of the Southwest with its intriguing fusion of cultural history, stunning landscapes, and traditional roadside attractions.

Arizona

From the Painted Desert to the Grand Canyon: Top Sites

Route 66 through Arizona is renowned for its breathtaking scenery, which includes the breathtaking Grand Canyon and the vibrant Painted Desert. This stretch of Route 66 through Arizona is among the most picturesque and culturally diverse because of the historic tiny towns, oddball roadside attractions, and breathtaking scenery that one may find there.

Holbrook, Arizona

Holbrook is a center of nostalgia for Route 66 and the entrance to the Petrified Forest:

- **Wigwam Motel**: Known as one of the most recognizable motels on Route 66, the Wigwam Motel offers classic, quirky Route 66 experiences with its teepee-shaped rooms.
- **Petrified Forest National Park**: Located a short distance from Holbrook, this park boasts breathtaking scenery featuring petrified wood, prehistoric fossils, and vivid desert hues. You have to take a drive through the Painted Desert.

Winslow, Arizona

Winslow provides a link to pop culture and the attractiveness of Route 66:

- **Standing on the Corner Park**: Named for the Eagles song "Take It Easy," this park has a mural that contains the song's well-known line and a life-sized

bronze statue. For aficionados of both music and Route 66, it's an enjoyable and picturesque stopover.
- The **La Posada Hotel** is an architectural marvel that offers guests a glimpse into the opulence of early 20th-century rail travel and the history of Route 66. It is a beautifully restored Harvey House hotel.

Flagstaff, Arizona

Flagstaff is a thriving city that provides access to neighboring natural beauties as well as the history of Route 66:

- **Museum Club**: Also referred to as "The Zoo," this famed Route 66 relic is a historic roadhouse and nightclub that provides live music and a window into Arizona's Western past.
- **Lowell Observatory**: One of the oldest astronomical observatories in the United States, Lowell Observatory is only a short drive from Route 66 and provides tourists with the opportunity to explore the stars and discover Arizona's scientific accomplishments.

Arizona's Seligman

Seligman is a tiny town with a lot of character for Route 66:

- **Delgadillo's Snow Cap Drive-In**: Visitors taking Route 66 should make time to see this eccentric, vintage diner. The Snow Cap, which was founded by Angel Delgadillo, a major player in the preservation of Route 66, offers burgers, milkshakes, and lots of laughs.
- **Seligman Historic District**: Full of vintage automobiles, neon signs, and ancient motels that take

you back to the glory of the Mother Road, Seligman is recognized as the cradle of Route 66's rebirth.

Grand Canyon National Park, Arizona

When going through Arizona, even if it's not directly on Route 66, you must take a detour to see the Grand Canyon:

- **Grand Canyon Village**: This historic hamlet, situated on the South Rim, provides breathtaking views, hiking trails, and cultural displays that highlight the geology and history of one of nature's wonders.

Driving Routes and What to Expect

- **Route Information**: Without taking into account detours to the Grand Canyon, a trip down Arizona's Route 66, which spans around 250 miles, can take four to five hours.
- Views of wide desert vistas, colorful rock formations, and tiny villages that have managed to maintain Route 66's history and culture are among the scenic and historical insights to be gained.

A great combination of scenic beauty, nostalgic stops, and the chance to visit one of the most well-known road trip locations worldwide can be found along Arizona's Route 66.

California

The End of the Road: Los Angeles and Beyond

Route 66 ends in California, where it heads west to the Pacific Ocean and culminates in the thriving metropolis of Los

Angeles. California offers an incredible way to cap out the Route 66 adventure, from the bustling cities of Los Angeles to the desolate expanses of the Mojave.

Barstow, California

The desert town of Barstow is steeped in the history and culture of Route 66:

- **Route 66 Mother Road Museum**: Housed in the historic Casa del Desierto Harvey House, this museum features a collection of vintage vehicles, signage, and images that perfectly encapsulate the spirit of the Mother Road.
- **Calico Ghost Town**: Just outside Barstow, Calico Ghost Town gives a view into California's mining past, with rebuilt buildings and stores that take tourists back to the 1880s.

San Bernardino, California

Some of the most famous locations along Route 66 are found in San Bernardino:

- **Original McDonald's Site and Museum:** Situated on the location of the original McDonald's, this museum provides an intriguing glimpse into the modest beginnings of what grew to become one of the biggest fast-food chains in the world.
- **Wigwam Motel**: Located in San Bernardino, this iconic teepee-shaped motel along Route 66 provides a nostalgic getaway and a quintessential Route 66 photo opportunity.

Pasadena, California

Pasadena provides a blend of culture, architecture, and history:

- **The Colorado Street Bridge** also referred to as the "Suicide Bridge," is a magnificent historic bridge that provides amazing views of Pasadena and has come to symbolize the city's Route 66 legacy.
- **Old Town Pasadena**: This bustling neighborhood allows tourists an opportunity to take in the rich culture and history of the city. It is home to several stores, eateries, and historic structures.

Santa Monica, California

Santa Monica is where the Pacific Ocean begins and Route 66 ends:

- **Santa Monica Pier**: Located at the official end of Route 66, the Santa Monica Pier is a busy tourist attraction with restaurants, rides at amusement parks, and breathtaking views of the ocean. It's the ideal location to enjoy finishing your Route 66 adventure.
- The **End of the Trail Sign**, which is situated at the pier and signifies the official end of Route 66, is an ideal opportunity to capture a photo to remember your journey across America.

Driving Routes and What to Expect:

- **Route details:** Barstow to Santa Monica is approximately 315 miles away on California Route 66, and the trip takes 4 to 5 hours.
- **Historical and Scenic Insights:** You'll witness desert and urban environments in addition to the

well-known Route 66 sites that bring you to the Pacific Ocean.

This historic adventure comes to a fitting finale on the California section of Route 66, which combines the excitement of traveling to the West Coast with the grandeur of the desert.

Chapter 5 . Historical Sites and Museums

Route 66 Museums

Exploring the rich history preserved in the museums along Route 66 is just as important as the travel itself. These museums enhance your travel along America's most famous route while preserving the tales, artifacts, and spirit of the Mother Road. They provide a window into the past.

Route 66 Association Hall of Fame & Museum (Pontiac, Illinois)

- 110 W Howard St., Pontiac, IL 61764 is the address.
- Admission is free, but donations are accepted.
- **Route**: About a 100-mile trip from Chicago via I-55 S, situated in downtown Pontiac, right off historic Route 66.
- **Directions**: Take IL-116 to W Howard St. after getting off I-55 S. Parking is accessible near the museum.

Why It's Unique: With a collection of artifacts from the companies and tourists who made the Route 66 Hall of Fame & Museum famous, it provides an immersive experience. Highlights include paintings and antique cars that offer guests a clear picture of Route 66's glory days. The museum is well-known for its outside "Wall Dogs" mural, which has gained popularity as an Instagram-worthy location and adds a vibrant story to the history of this street.

Route 66 Museum (Kingman, Arizona)

- 120 W Andy Devine Ave, Kingman, AZ 86401 is the address.
- **Price**: $4 for adults, $2 for kids (ages 7 to 11), and free for kids under six
- **Route**: Situated directly on Route 66, the museum can be reached by car from neighboring communities such as Oatman and Williams, Arizona.
- **How to Get There**: Take I-40 to the Andy Devine Avenue exit (number 48). It is simple to discover the museum because it is situated along the same section of historic Route 66.

Why It's Unique: Housed in the historic Powerhouse building, this museum is not only a great spot to learn about the history of Route 66 but also a noteworthy landmark in and of itself. It discusses the building of Route 66, how travelers were affected by the Great Depression, and how the route played a part in American migration. Photographs, relics, and an amazing collection of vintage cars are also on display. It is especially important to people who are interested in the more difficult part of the road because of its comprehensive displays regarding the travel through the Mojave Desert during the Dust Bowl.

National Route 66 Museum (Elk City, Oklahoma)

- 2717 W 3rd St, Elk City, OK 73644 is the address.
- The price is $5 for adults, $4 for seniors, and $2 for kids (six to sixteen).
- **Route**: Directly off of I-40 on W 3rd Street. It's conveniently located as you head into Amarillo, Texas, at a distance of roughly 115 miles west of Oklahoma City.

- **How to Get There**: From I-40, take exit 32 and head west on W 3rd Street for approximately two miles. Parking is abundant throughout the museum complex.

Why It's Unique: The National Route 66 Museum honors the tiny towns and villages along the route in addition to the road itself. With life-sized reconstructions of 1950s diners, motels, and vintage cars, it offers a nostalgic trip. The Old Town Museum and the Farm & Ranch Museum are two more exhibitions in the Elk City Museum Complex that provide a more comprehensive historical backdrop of life in America during the heyday of Route 66's notoriety. It is a multifaceted event that blends the history of Route 66 on a local and national level.

Oklahoma Route 66 Museum (Clinton, Oklahoma)

- **Address**: Clinton, Oklahoma, 73601, 2229 W Gary Blvd.
- The price is $7 for adults, $5 for seniors, $4 for kids (ages 6 to 18), and free for kids under 6.
- **Route**: This museum is located exactly along Route 66 in the center of Oklahoma, on Gary Boulevard, approximately 85 miles west of Oklahoma City.
- **How to Get There**: Take W Gary Blvd., exit 65A off of I-40. The museum is only a short drive off the main highway; simply follow the signage.

Why It's Unique: Often regarded as the greatest Route 66 museum, this place showcases the road's whole history from its creation in 1926 to its deactivation in 1985. The road's development is depicted in exhibits organized by decade at the museum, which also features vintage images, signage, and

67

restored vehicles. A stroll around the museum is akin to peering into a time capsule, as its exhibits portray the evolving nature of tourism and culture along Route 66. Your visit will feel more hands-on thanks to its interactive exhibitions, which include a 1950s-style diner and a historically realistic petrol station.

California Route 66 Museum (Victorville, California)

- 16825 D St., Victorville, CA 92395 is the address.
- Admission is free, while donations are welcome.
- **Route**: On the final section of Route 66 before arriving in Los Angeles, close to the Mojave Desert.
- **How to Get There**: Travel a few miles on D Street after taking I-15 N to exit 153A. Situated directly on Route 66, the museum is easily visible from the highway.

Why It's Unique: The California Route 66 Museum displays items from the western end of the route, including neon signs, vintage automobiles, and a cafe from the 1950s. This museum captures the lively and carefree vibe of Route 66 and is well-known for its peculiar and interactive exhibits, which include a VW bus that you can get inside and take pictures of. Offering a jubilant look at how the highway affected the state and American car culture, it's one of the last major museums before Route 66 ends in Santa Monica.

In addition to offering visitors fascinating exhibits and an understanding of the communities and cultures that flourished along this famous highway, each of these museums along Route 66 offers a distinctive piece of history. These museums are a must-see while traveling Route 66, regardless of your interest in neon signs, classic cars, or Dust Bowl history.

Historical Markers and Monuments Along Route 66

Route 66 is a living monument to American history, much more than just a route. Many historical markers and monuments that honor important occasions, figures, and points in time that influenced the road and the American experience as a whole can be found along the route. Every one of them provides visitors with a more profound connection to history, whether it is through memorials commemorating the Dust Bowl migration or historical cafes and motels.

The Cyrus Avery Route 66 Memorial Bridge (Tulsa, Oklahoma)

- 11th St. Bridge, Tulsa, OK 74104 is the address.
- **Route**: Following the historic Route 66 layout, it is situated on the east side of Tulsa's downtown.
- **Directions**: Travel on I-244 E and get off at 7th Street. To reach the bridge over 11th Street, follow the signage.

Why It's Unique: Cyrus Avery, dubbed the "Father of Route 66," played a key role in the construction of the roadway, and this monument honors his contributions. Once a section of the original Route 66 path, the historic bridge is now accompanied by a monument that includes a bronze figure of Avery along with a vintage 1920s vehicle. The monument honors Avery's contribution to the realization of Route 66 and highlights Tulsa's significance as a major hub along the route.

The Cadillac Ranch (Amarillo, Texas)

- **Address**: 79124, Amarillo, Texas, I-40 Frontage Road
- **Route**: Cadillac Ranch is located just outside of Amarillo and is reachable by I-40, a contemporary roadway that, in many areas of Texas, took the place of Route 66.
- **Directions**: Take I-40 to exit 62A, then follow the frontage road to the destination. There is parking close to Cadillac Ranch, and the property is visible from the highway.

Why It's Special: Cadillac Ranch is one of the most recognizable structures on Route 66, despite not being an official historical marker. Designed as a piece of public art in 1974, the ranch showcases ten partially submerged Cadillacs that have been individually spray-painted by guests. It is a must-see for anyone wishing to explore the quirky side of Route 66 and has come to represent the free-spirited, artistic attitude of the route throughout the years. Bring your spray paint and get creative with the cars—visitors are welcome to do so, turning the location into a dynamic work of Route 66 art.

The Blue Whale of Catoosa (Catoosa, Oklahoma)

- **Address**: Catoosa, OK 74015, 2600 Rte 66
- Situated east of Tulsa, in Catoosa, on the north side of Route 66.
- **How to Get There**: From Tulsa, travel for approximately fifteen minutes on Route 66. There is parking accessible on-site, making the Blue Whale easy to miss.

Why It's Unique: Originally constructed as a charming roadside attraction in the early 1970s, the Blue Whale of Catoosa has grown to become one of Route 66's most well-known landmarks. This 80-foot-long whale, which was once part of a swimming hole and picnic area, continues to draw tourists from all over the world. Children love it because of its upbeat, family-friendly atmosphere, while adults find its nostalgic appeal appealing. The location is a representation of the wacky side attractions that once attracted families to Route 66.

The Will Rogers Monument (Claremore, Oklahoma)

- 1720 W Will Rogers Blvd., Claremore, OK 74017 is the address.
- **Route**: The memorial may be found in Claremore, right off Route 66, near the Will Rogers Memorial Museum.
- **How to Get There**: From Tulsa, travel approximately 30 miles north on Route 66. To reach the memorial, take the W Will Rogers Blvd. exit and heed the directions.

Why It's Special: Oklahoma was home to Will Rogers, one of the country's most adored comedians and actors. Located just off Route 66, this memorial and museum honoring his life and contributions make for a convenient and poignant stop for tourists. The monument outside recognizes Rogers' contributions to American culture, and the museum features displays of his films, wit, and political criticism. Because of Rogers' impact on America in the early 20th century, this monument is worth stopping by for thought when traveling Route 66.

The Standin' on the Corner Park (Winslow, Arizona)

- The address is Winslow, AZ 86047, 100 N Kinsley Ave.
- **Route**: Located just along Route 66 in the heart of Winslow.
- **Directions**: Take Route 66 and drive till you get to Kinsley Avenue. There is parking close to the park in downtown Winslow.

Why It's Special: Though rooted in pop culture rather than history, this monument is a testament to how deeply Route 66 has embedded itself in American music and folklore. Inspired by the Eagles' famous song "Take It Easy," Standin' on the Corner Park features a statue of a man with a guitar and a mural that commemorates the song's famous line about "standin' on a corner in Winslow, Arizona." For those who enjoy music, this is a fun stop that blends Americana with the history of rock & roll.

Route 66 Monument (Rolla, Missouri)

- 1008 Kingshighway, Rolla, MO 65401 is the address.
- **Route**: Found on Kingshighway, following Route 66's original course through Rolla.
- **How to Get There**: Take Route 66 and head toward Rolla's Kingshighway, following the signs. There is parking close by, making the monument conveniently accessible.

Why It's Unique: This monument honors Rolla's role as an important Route 66 station. The enormous artwork made of stone and metal honors the spirit of the highway and its function in tying the nation together. The Rolla monument is a remarkable piece of modern art that pays homage to Route 66 by fusing elements of classic Americana with contemporary design. For those looking to document the spirit of their trip, it's also a fantastic chance to take pictures.

Chain of Rocks Bridge (St. Louis, Missouri)

- 10820 Riverview Dr., St. Louis, MO 63137 is the address.
- **Route**: This bridge, which spans the Mississippi River, follows the historic Route 66 route to link Illinois and Missouri.
- **How to Get There**: Head toward the Chain of Rocks Bridge by following the signs on I-270 to Riverview Drive. There is parking close to the pedestrian walkway's entrance.

Why It's Unique: Known for its unusual 22-degree curve in the middle, the Chain of Rocks Bridge is one of the most well-known bridges on Route 66. It was first opened in 1929 and remained a vital Mississippi River crossing until the 1960s. The bridge is now accessible to bikers and pedestrians, providing breathtaking views over the Missouri River and the city skyline of St. Louis. Crossing this historical monument seems like a real link to the millions of people who came before you on their trip west.

Route 66 Park (St. Louis, Missouri)

- **Address**: St. Louis, MO 63114, 9728 St. Charles Rock Road
- **Route**: Route 66 Park, a leisurely stop along the way, is situated just off Route 66 in St. Louis.

- **How to Get There**: Take the St. Charles Rock Road exit off of I-270 S, which leads to the park.

Why It's Unique: Route 66 Park honors the road that influenced a great deal of American history and goes beyond being just a park. The park provides a serene setting for visitors to consider their journey, complete with picnic spaces, strolling pathways, and historical signage on Route 66. Historical monuments honoring Route 66's significance in tying the Midwest to the rest of the nation may also be found there.

More than just roadside attractions, these historical monuments and memorials serve as reminders of the people, occasions, and cultures that made Route 66 iconic. Every one of them gives visitors the ability to travel through time, establish a connection with the past, and comprehend the significance of America's Mother Road on a deeper level.

Chapter 6. Dining and Local Eats

Iconic Diners and Cafes

The cuisine of Route 66 is almost as important as its historical sites. More than just a place to eat, the vintage cafes and restaurants along this famous street give a flavor of American culinary heritage. These famous restaurants, which range from retro diners with neon signage to welcoming cafes offering local specialties, are an essential component of the Route 66 experience. Here's a deeper look at a few of the Mother Road's must-eat locations:

Lou Mitchell's (Chicago, Illinois)

- 565 W Jackson Blvd., Chicago, IL 60661 is the address.
- **Route**: Situated close to the beginning of Route 66 in downtown Chicago.
- **How to Get There**: Several public transit choices make it easy to get from the central Chicago area.

Why It's Unique: A treasured Route 66 institution since its opening in 1923, Lou Mitchell's is a quintessential American restaurant. The diner, which is well-known for its substantial breakfasts and retro appeal, creates a nostalgic atmosphere with its classic furnishings and welcoming staff. Their renowned cinnamon rolls, biscuits & gravy, and fluffy pancakes are among their signature meals. Families and tourists alike love it because of the special touches it offers, including free donut holes and milk for the kids.

Costs: Depending on your options, plan to pay between $10 and $20 per person for a meal.

The Route 66 Diner (Barstow, California)

- 1611 E Main St., Barstow, CA 92311 is the address.
- **Route**: Located along the old line of Route 66 in Barstow, California.
- **How to Get There**: The diner is conveniently located just off I-15 and is reachable from the interstate.

Why It's Unique: With its vintage decor and traditional diner meals, the Route 66 Diner perfectly embodies mid-century Americana. It gives a genuine Route 66 atmosphere with its neon signage, checkered floors, and chrome fittings. The menu has specialty products like the "Route 66 Burger" and homemade pie in addition to traditional diner fare including burgers, fries, and milkshakes. The diner is the ideal place to experience the glory days of road travel because of its classic ambiance and welcoming staff.**Costs**: An average meal for one person is between $10 and $25.

The Blue Swallow Motel Cafe (Tucumcari, New Mexico)

- 100 E Route 66 Blvd., Tucumcari, NM 88401 is the address.
- Situated in Tucumcari, New Mexico, along Route 66.
- **How to Get There**: Located inside the Blue Swallow Motel, a famed Route 66 relic, is the cafe.

Why It's Unique: Though the Blue Swallow Motel Cafe is best recognized as a historic motel, it also provides a warm dining experience with a nod to old Route 66. The cafe features a vintage appeal that mirrors the motel and serves comfort food and traditional American breakfasts. The menu features traditional diner fare along with hearty breakfast options like pancakes and omelets. The cafe's allure is increased by its association with the Blue Swallow Motel, a revered Route 66 landmark.

Costs: Budget between $10 and $20 for each person.

The 66 Diner (Albuquerque, New Mexico)

- 1405 Central Ave NE, Albuquerque, NM 87106 is the address.
- **Route**: Situated along Central Avenue, which travels through Albuquerque along the route of the former Route 66.
- **How to Get There**: Central Albuquerque and I-40 make it easy to get to.

Why It's Unique: With its vintage 1950s design and retro ambiance, The 66 Diner is a bright and colorful ode to the Route 66 period. The restaurant is well-known for its wide selection of traditional American fare, which includes thick breakfasts, milkshakes, and hamburgers. The diner's friendly staff and classic jukebox add to its nostalgic vibe. The "Route 66 Burger" and the "Rockin' Strawberry Shake" are two of the most well-liked dishes.

Costs: A meal for one person usually costs between $10 and $20.

The Munger Moss Motel Cafe (Lebanon, Missouri)

- **Address**: 1051 E Route 66, Lebanon, MO 65536

- **Route**: Situated in Lebanon, Missouri, on Route 66.
- **How to Get There**: The cafe is conveniently located on Route 66, making it a convenient destination for travelers.

Why It's Unique: The Munger Moss Motel, another recognizable Route 66 landmark, has a cafe serving traditional American diner fare. The cafe offers a range of classic fare, such as burgers, sandwiches, and breakfast classics. For fans of Route 66, the nostalgic charm and historical significance of the Munger Moss Motel make it an essential stop. The motel itself enhances the whole experience with its retro signage and immaculate exterior.

Costs: The average person should budget between $10 and $20 for a meal.

The Red Dog Cafe (Kingman, Arizona)

- The address is Kingman, Arizona 86401, 411 E Andy Devine Ave.
- **Route**: Situated in Kingman, Arizona, along Route 66.
- **Directions**: The cafe is located on Kingman's main Route 66 thoroughfare.

Why It's Unique: With its vintage furnishings and welcoming ambiance, the Red Dog Cafe provides a distinctive Route 66 eating experience. A variety of American comfort foods, such as burgers, baked pies, and hearty breakfasts, are available on the cafe's menu. Travelers seeking a traditional diner experience frequently visit the Red Dog Cafe because of its retro charm and ties to the Route 66 past.

Costs: A meal for one person usually costs between $10 and $20.

The Cozy Dog Drive In (Springfield, Illinois)

- 2935 S. 6th St., Springfield, IL 62703 is the address.
- **Route**: Situated near Springfield on the iconic Route 66.
- **How to Get There**: From I-55, take the 6th Street exit and go south to reach the location.

Why It's Special: This diner, which has been a Route 66 mainstay since the 1940s, is well-known for creating the "Cozy Dog" on a stick. The Cozy Dog Drive-In continues to serve its namesake dish—hot dogs on a stick, dipped in cornmeal batter and fried—along with other American mainstays like burgers and fries. The Cozy Dog Drive-In is a popular destination for Route 66 travelers because of its nostalgic atmosphere and historical significance.

Costs: Budget between $10 and $15 for each person.

The Midpoint Cafe (Adelanto, Texas)

- **Address**: Adrian, Texas, 79001; 208 W Main St.
- **Route**: Adrian, Texas, at the middle of Route 66.
- **How to Get There**: Conveniently located near Adrian on Route 66, just a short drive off Highway 287.

Why It's Unique: With its roadside charm and retro decor, this cafe, which bills itself as the "middle of Route 66," delivers a singular experience. In addition to serving traditional diner fare including burgers, sandwiches, and pies, The Midpoint Cafe has items related to Route 66. The cafe is a unique stop for travelers wishing to commemorate reaching the halfway point of the Mother Road because of its unique position and historical significance.

Costs: A meal for one person usually costs between $10 and $20.

These recognizable cafes and diners are more than just spots to eat; they are essential components of the Route 66 experience, each providing a nostalgic taste of American history. These restaurants offer a delectable way to reconnect with history and taste the cuisines that have been treasured by generations of visitors as you go along the Mother Road.

Regional Specialties and Local Favorites

You'll come across a wide range of regional delicacies and neighborhood favorites that showcase the distinctive culinary customs of every state as you go along Route 66. Every part of the country offers a unique flavor of Route 66, ranging from substantial Midwestern meals to Southwestern delicacies. Here's a list of some of the local favorites and must-try regional specialties along the Mother Road:

- **Illinois: Deep-Dish Pizza and Italian Beef**

Deep-Dish Pizza:

- **Where to Go**: Chicago, IL's Lou Malnati's Pizzeria
- 1120 N State St., Chicago, IL 60610 is the address.

What to Expect: Deep-dish pizza, which is Chicago's specialty, is distinguished by layers of cheese, savory tomato sauce, and toppings on top of a thick, buttery dough. The storied Lou Malnati's pizza is renowned for its real deep-dish experience. You can anticipate a thick, decadent pizza with a crunchy crust, melted cheese, and a hearty tomato sauce.

Italian Beef Sandwich:

- **Where to Try**: Chicago, IL's Al's Beef
- 1079 W Taylor St., Chicago, IL 60607 is the address.

What to Expect: A Chicago tradition, the Italian beef sandwich consists of thinly sliced roast beef served on a crusty Italian toast and cooked in a flavorful broth. This famous sandwich is best enjoyed at Al's Beef, where it's frequently topped with sweet peppers and giardiniera, or spicy pickled veggies.

- **Missouri: Toasted Ravioli and BBQ**

Toasted Ravioli:

- **Where to Try**: The Hill in St. Louis, Missouri
- 1035 S. 10th St., St. Louis, MO 63104 is the address.

What to Expect: Deep-fried, breaded ravioli topped with marinara sauce is known as toasted ravioli, a St. Louis specialty. This inventive version of ravioli is ideal as an appetizer or snack because it has a crispy outside and a warm, cheesy filling.

St. Louis BBQ:

- Pappy's Smokehouse (St. Louis, MO) is the place to try.
- 3107 S Manchester Ave, St. Louis, MO 63139 is the address.

What to Expect: The distinctive tomato-based sauce and spare ribs of St. Louis-style barbecue are well-known. Famous for its smoked meats, Pappy's Smokehouse serves a variety of barbecue specialties with a deep, smokey flavor, such as succulent ribs, pulled pigs, and burnt ends.

- **Oklahoma: Chicken-Fried Steak and Fried Onion Burgers**

Chicken-Fried Steak:

- Cattlemen's Steakhouse in Oklahoma City is a good place to try.
- 1309 S Agnew Ave, Oklahoma City, OK 73108 is the address.

What to Expect: A Southern tradition, chicken-fried steak is made of breaded and fried beef steak, which is frequently served with gravy. Oklahoma City's legendary Cattlemen's Steakhouse is well-known for its substantial servings and authentic take on this well-loved meal.

Fried Onion Burger:

- Try Sid's Diner in El Reno, Oklahoma.
- 107 E Hwy 66, El Reno, OK 73036 is the address.

What to Expect: A beef patty topped with crispy, caramelized onions is the centerpiece of the beloved fried onion burger in the area. Since the 1950s, Sid's Diner has been providing customers with delicious juicy, savory burgers with a distinctive twist.

- **Texas: Tex-Mex and Barbecue Brisket**

Tex-Mex Cuisine:

- **Where to Go:** San Antonio, Texas's Mi Tierra Cafe y Panaderia
- 218 Produce Row, San Antonio, TX 78207 is the address.

What to Expect: American components are combined with Mexican tastes in Tex-Mex cooking. With its colorful decor and lively environment, Mi Tierra Cafe y Panaderia is a lively restaurant in San Antonio that serves traditional Tex-Mex fare including enchiladas, tamales, and sizzling fajitas.

Barbecue Brisket:

- Big Texan Steak Ranch (Amarillo, TX) is the place to try.
- **Address**: Amarillo, Texas 79118, 7701 I-40

What to Expect: Texas is well-known for its beef brisket and other forms of barbecue. The BBQ brisket at Big Texan Steak Ranch is well-known for being slow-cooked to perfection and comes with all the fixings. For lovers of BBQ, the restaurant is a must-visit because of its hefty quantities and rustic setting.

- **New Mexico: Green Chile and Sopapillas**

Green Chile:

- **Where to Go**: Santa Fe, New Mexico's The Shed
- 113 1/2 E Palace Ave, Santa Fe, NM 87501 is the address.

What to Expect: Known for their smoky and spicy flavor, green chiles are a mainstay of New Mexican cuisine. Offering a true flavor of New Mexico's culinary legacy, The Shed serves enchiladas and green chile stew among other dishes that feature green chile.

Sopapillas:

- Tia Sophia's is the place to try (Santa Fe, NM)
- 210 W San Francisco St., Santa Fe, NM 87501 is the address.

What to Expect: Sopapillas are fluffy, airy pastries that are typically eaten with honey or as a dessert. Delicious sopapillas are available at Tia Sophia's as a sweet way to end your meal. They're a light and airy delight that go well with New Mexican food.

- **Arizona: Navajo Tacos and Churros**

Navajo Tacos:

- **Where to Try**: El Charro Cafe (Tucson, AZ)
- 311 N Court Ave, Tucson, AZ 85701 is the address.

What to Expect: Traditionally, taco toppings including ground beef, beans, lettuce, and cheese are served atop fried bread-based Navajo tacos. This unusual meal, which combines flavors and textures to offer a taste of Native American and Southwestern fusion cuisine, is served at Tucson's famous El Charro Cafe.

Churros:

- **Where to Go**: Phoenix, Arizona's ChurroMania
- 725 E Bell Road, Phoenix, AZ 85022 is the address.

What to Expect: Churros, deep-fried pastries coated in cinnamon sugar, are a popular treat in Arizona. Traveling is the ideal time to indulge in Churro Mania's beautifully crispy and sweet snack, which comes in a range of flavors.

- **California: California Burritos and In-N-Out Burger**

California Burritos:

- **Where to Try**: San Diego, California's Lucha Libre Taco Shop
- 1810 W Washington St., San Diego, CA 92110 is the address.

What to Expect: A local staple, California burritos are usually stuffed with fries, salsa, cheese, and beef asada. Famous for its mouthwatering California burritos, Lucha Libre Taco Shop provides a satisfying combination of flavors in a sizable serving.

Burger from In-N-Out:

- **Where to Go**: Los Angeles, California's In-N-Out Burger
- **Address**: Various places in Los Angeles

What to Expect: The well-liked fast-food company In-N-Out Burger is well-known for its straightforward menu and fresh ingredients. With an emphasis on quality and flavor, the renowned "Double-Double" burger, animal-style fries, and milkshakes provide a traditional California eating experience.

Experience the varied gastronomic scene of Route 66 with these delectable regional delicacies and local favorites.

Travelers may enjoy a delectable voyage through the history and flavors of this famous American roadway, with each dish showcasing distinctive cultural influences and regional ingredients.

Chapter 7. Accommodation Options

Classic Motels and Hotels

Known as the "Main Street of America," Route 66 boasts a long history of vintage hotels and motels that have served tourists for many years. These lodgings offer a respite from the heat and a window into the nostalgic allure of mid-century America. Here's a guide to some of the iconic motels and hotels along Route 66, with information on their prices, history, and anticipated changes in 2025:

- **Illinois**

The Beverly Motel – Chicago, IL

- 4714 S Pulaski Road, Chicago, IL 60632 is the address.
- **Cost**: between $70 and $120 per night

What to Expect: The Beverly Motel, which is situated on Chicago's southern border, retains its classic retro ambiance thanks to its retro signage and uncomplicated lodging options. Travelers looking to see the Chicago region before embarking on their Route 66 adventure will find the motel to be a sensible option because of its tidy rooms and basic amenities. The Beverly's vintage charm and reasonable prices make for a nostalgic stay.

The Route 66 Inn – Springfield, IL

- 1800 N Dirksen Parkway, Springfield, IL 62702 is the address.
- **Cost each night**: $65 to $110.

What to Expect: With its retro decor and handy location, the Route 66 Inn in Springfield perfectly embodies the spirit of Route 66. The hotel is well located to explore Springfield's historical sites, such as the Abraham Lincoln Presidential Library and Museum, and offers cozy accommodations with contemporary conveniences. Anticipate a comfortable stay with a hint of vintage Route 66 charm.

- Missouri

The Wagon Wheel Motel – Cuba, MO

- 901 E Washington St., Cuba, MO 65453 is the address.
- **Cost**: $80 to $130 per evening

What to Expect: The Wagon Wheel Motel is a famous historic Route 66 landmark that has retained its neon signage and unique mid-century decor. The motel offers comfortable, retro-style rooms with contemporary amenities including flat-screen TVs and Wi-Fi. The Wagon Wheel is well-known for its welcoming staff and nostalgic ambiance, which capture the vintage essence of Route 66.

The 66 Motel – St. Louis, MO

- 7216 S Broadway St, St. Louis, MO 63111 is the address.
- **Cost per night**: $75 to $115

What to Expect: The 66 Motel, which is situated in the southern region of St. Louis, has vintage furnishings and iconic Route 66 characteristics. Travelers who want to explore the city will find the motel to be a convenient option, offering simple lodgings with basic amenities. Because of its affordable

88

prices and charming antique appeal, it's a well-liked option for those who want to honor the Route 66 legacy.

- **Oklahoma**

The Rock Cafe – Stroud, OK

- **Address**: 114 W Main St, Stroud, OK 74079
- **Cost**: $140 to $90 each night

What to Expect: The Rock Cafe, although best known as a vintage Route 66 diner, also has comfortable, retro-themed rooms available for overnight stays. A unique combination of dining and accommodation experiences is offered by The Rock Cafe, which is known for its historical connection to Route 66 and its unusual design from the 1930s. Visitors can take in the vintage diner ambiance while learning about the history of Route 66 in the area.

The Route 66 Inn – Clinton, OK

- **Address**: 820 W Gary Blvd, Clinton, OK 73601
- **Cost**: between $70 and $120 per night

What to Expect: Conveniently placed for travelers exploring this historic section, the Route 66 Inn in Clinton offers traditional Route 66 decor. The motel provides tidy, cozy rooms with all the conveniences you might want in a friendly environment. For those who love Route 66, its retro design and close accessibility to nearby sites make it a great option.

- **Texas**

The Big Texan Motel – Amarillo, TX

- **Address**: Amarillo, Texas 79118, 7701 I-40
- **Cost**: between $80 and $140 per night

What to Expect: This motel, which is next to the well-known Big Texan Steak Ranch, features traditional Route 66 decor and retro furnishings with a vintage Western motif. The Big Texan Motel offers cozy accommodations, a sizable pool area, and quick access to the steakhouse's entertainment and dining choices. The ambiance has a contemporary feel while retaining the allure of mid-century America.

The Route 66 Inn – Amarillo, TX

- **Address**: Amarillo, Texas 79104, 2900 E I-40
- **Cost**: $60 to $110 per lodging

What to Expect: This motel with a Route 66 theme provides affordable lodging with a nostalgic feel. The accommodations are basic but cozy, with vintage furnishings and standard conveniences. Its convenient position close to major roads and nearby attractions makes it a great option for Route 66 tourists seeking a comfortable and traditional place to stay.

- New Mexico

The El Rancho Hotel – Gallup, NM

- **Address**: Gallup, New Mexico 87301, 1000 E Highway 66
- **Cost**: $90 to $150 per lodging

What to Expect: The El Rancho Hotel has a rich history that dates back to the 1930s and is a historic Route 66 monument. Recognized for its historic Hollywood ties and southwestern design, the hotel offers cozy accommodations with a touch of nostalgia. Visitors can take in the hotel's distinctive atmosphere and learn about its historical significance, which includes its status as a popular hangout for movie stars.

The Blue Swallow Motel – Tucumcari, NM

- **Address**: Tucumcari, New Mexico 88401, 815 E Route 66 Blvd.
- **Cost per night**: $75 to $125

What to Expect: Known for its traditional design and neon signs from the past, the Blue Swallow Motel is a well-known Route 66 landmark. The motel offers classic rooms with contemporary conveniences in a cozy setting. Its preservation of mid-century elegance and its significance as a Route 66 emblem make it a must-visit for fans and travelers.

- **Arizona**

The Historic Route 66 Motel – Kingman, AZ

- 116 E Andy Devine Ave, Kingman, AZ 86401 is the address.
- **Cost**: $80 to $130 per evening

What to Expect: Offering retro-style accommodations with a typical Route 66 vibe, the Historic Route 66 Motel is located in Kingman. The motel includes genuine 1950s decor and delivers modern conveniences while keeping its historical charm. It's a great place to stop and explore Kingman and the neighboring areas because of its central location.

The Best Western Plus – Flagstaff, AZ

- 3601 E Lockett Road, Flagstaff, AZ 86004 is the address.
- **Cost**: $100 to $160 per lodging

What to Expect: This Best Western Plus in Flagstaff offers cozy lodging that combines traditional and modern design elements, even if it's not a Route 66 motel. The hotel is a great starting point for visiting Route 66 and neighboring sites like the Grand Canyon, and it has modern facilities including a pool and free breakfast.

- **California**

The Wigwam Motel – San Bernardino, CA

- **Address**: San Bernardino, California, 92410, 2728 W Foothill Blvd.
- **Cost**: $140 to $90 each night

What to Expect: The Wigwam Motel provides a distinctive and nostalgic Route 66 experience with its recognizable wigwam-shaped accommodations. This iconic roadside attraction, which dates back to the 1950s, offers themed rooms with contemporary conveniences and nostalgic décor. On the last stretch of your Route 66 adventure, the motel is a noteworthy stop due to its unique appearance and historical significance.

The Hotel Constance – Los Angeles, CA

- 222 W 7th St., Los Angeles, CA 90014 is the address.
- **Price**: $130 to $200 per lodging

What to Expect: The Hotel Constance, which is situated in downtown Los Angeles, combines traditional elegance with contemporary comfort. Even while it's not exactly on Route 66, its closeness to the highway's terminus makes it an easy option for travelers coming to the end of their trip. The hotel offers amenities that support both leisure and exploration of the exciting LA region, together with chic rooms and a restaurant.

These vintage motels and hotels along Route 66 provide a nostalgic trip down memory lane, capturing the allure and rich history of the country's most well-known highway. Every lodging offers a different experience, be it the historical significance, the retro atmosphere, or just a cozy spot to crash while traveling the Mother Road.

Unique Places to Stay on Route 66

In addition to providing passengers with an opportunity to travel through America's heartland, Route 66, the famous highway that connects Chicago to Santa Monica, also gives a chance to stay in some rather unusual places. These distinctive lodging options, which range from quirky motels to historic inns, provide your Route 66 journey an extra dose of charm and nostalgia. Here is a list of some of the most unique accommodations you can find along the way:

- **Illinois**

The Henry Ford Museum – Dearborn, IL

- 20900 Oakwood Blvd., Dearborn, MI 48124 is the address.
- **Cost**: $100 to $150 each evening

What to Expect: The Henry Ford Museum provides a unique overnight experience through its special events and exhibitions, even if it is not a standard lodging option. The museum, which is only a short drive from Chicago's Route 66 starting point, offers an immersive experience of American invention and history with its vast collection of automotive and industrial items.

The Palmer House Hilton – Chicago, IL

- 17 E Monroe St., Chicago, IL 60603 is the address.
- **Cost**: $200 to $350 per evening

What to Expect: The Palmer House Hilton, one of Chicago's iconic hotels, offers a luxurious and historical experience. The hotel, which opened in 1871, is a remarkable setting to begin your Route 66 adventure because of its exquisite architecture and sumptuous décor. Its central Chicago location gives it an ideal starting point for discovering the rich cultural and historical sites of the city.

- **Missouri**

The Route 66 Hotel and Conference Center – Springfield, MO

- **Address**: 65803 Springfield, MO, 2610 N Kansas Expressway
- **Cost**: $80 to $130 per evening

What to Expect: With its vintage furnishings and artifacts, this hotel offers a unique Route 66-themed experience. For those who love the Mother Road, the hotel offers vintage-inspired accommodations, a classic diner, and a range of memorabilia related to the route. Access to nearby attractions is made simple by its handy Springfield location.

The Elms Hotel and Spa – Excelsior Springs, MO

- The address is Excelsior Springs, MO 64024, 401 Regent St.
- **Cost**: $150 to $250 per lodging

What to Expect: The Elms Hotel is a historic spa hotel that offers a distinctive fusion of luxury and relaxation, just a short drive from Route 66. Distinguished by its opulent architecture and well-known spa offerings, the hotel offers an elegant haven with a dash of old-world charm. During its lengthy history, The Elms has welcomed many well-known visitors.

- **Oklahoma**

The Rock Café – Stroud, OK

- **Address**: Stroud, Oklahoma, 74079, 114 W Main St.
- **Expense**: $140 to $90 each night

What to Expect: The Rock Café, while mostly a diner, provides a distinctive accommodation experience with its throwback rooms and Route 66 vibe. Travelers can experience a nostalgic environment at the café because of its historical relevance and retro decor. Remaining here provides a unique experience of lodging and traditional Route 66 eating in an opulent historical environment.

The Blue Dome Diner – Tulsa, OK

- 324 E 11th St, Tulsa, OK 74119 is the address.
- **Cost**: between $70 and $120 per night

What to Expect: The Blue Dome Diner in Tulsa, despite not being a motel, provides a unique Route 66 experience with its neon signage and decor from the 1950s. Before moving on to adjacent lodging, it's a terrific place for a memorable dinner and picture opportunity. Its vintage charm encapsulates the spirit of eating on Route 66.

- **Texas**

The Big Texan Steak Ranch and Motel – Amarillo, TX

- **Address**: Amarillo, Texas 79118, 7701 I-40
- **Cost**: between $80 and $140 per night

What to Expect: Offering a distinctively Western experience, the Big Texan Motel is situated next to the well-known Big Texan Steak Ranch. The steakhouse's renowned 72-ounce steak challenge is available to guests, and the motel's rooms are furnished with a Texan flair. This stay combines nostalgia on Route 66 with hearty Texas cooking.

The Midland Hotel – Midland, TX

- **Address**: Midland, Texas 79701, 201 W Wall St.
- **Cost**: $90 to $150 per lodging

What to Expect: The Midland Hotel, which is situated in Midland's downtown, has early 20th-century architecture that gives it a historic feel. The hotel offers a distinctive stay along your Texas Route 66 adventure because it combines traditional charm with contemporary conveniences.

- **New Mexico**

New Mexico

The El Rancho Hotel – Gallup, NM

- **Address**: Gallup, New Mexico 87301, 1000 E Highway 66
- **Cost**: $90 to $150 per lodging

What to Expect: The El Rancho Hotel is well-known for its Southwestern décor and connections to Hollywood. With its traditional Native American-inspired décor and antique furnishings, this historic hotel—which has played host to several well-known movie stars—offers a unique experience. For anyone looking for a mix of cultural diversity and Route 66 heritage, it's a must-visit.

The Blue Swallow Motel – Tucumcari, NM

- **Address**: Tucumcari, New Mexico 88401, 815 E Route 66 Blvd.
- **Cost per night**: $75 to $125

What to Expect: The retro-style rooms and recognizable neon signs make the Blue Swallow Motel stand out. Enjoy a genuine and unforgettable stay with its well-preserved mid-century design and traditional Route 66 charm. The motel is a favorite among Route 66 tourists because of its cozy atmosphere and vintage appeal.

- **Arizona**

The Wigwam Motel – San Bernardino, CA

- **Address**: San Bernardino, California, 92410, 2728 W Foothill Blvd.
- **Cost**: $140 to $90 each night

What to Expect: The Wigwam Motel provides a unique and nostalgic Route 66 experience with its rooms designed like wigwams. The motel, which dates back to the 1950s, offers themed rooms with contemporary conveniences and retro décor. It's a noteworthy stop on the last stretch of your Route 66 tour because of its iconic appearance and historical significance.

The Kingman Route 66 Motel – Kingman, AZ

- 116 E Andy Devine Ave, Kingman, AZ 86401 is the address.
- **Cost**: $80 to $130 per evening

What to Expect: With its retro rooms and vintage decor, this hotel delivers a typical Route 66 ambiance. The Kingman Route 66 Motel delivers modern conveniences while keeping its vintage charm. Its Kingman location gives it an ideal starting point for visiting the city and the nearby Route 66 attractions.

These distinctive lodging options along Route 66 offer more than just a place to relax; they also provide a historical glimpse and a hint of nostalgia, making your trip down America's Mother Road an unforgettable and enlightening one. Every lodging option adds a unique charm to your journey by reflecting the rich history of Route 66.

Chapter 8. Outdoor Adventures

Scenic Drives and Natural Attractions

Not only can you relive history when traveling along Route 66, but you can also take in some of the most stunning natural scenery and picturesque drives in the country. Traveling the Mother Road will introduce you to a wide variety of outdoor experiences that highlight the splendor of the American Southwest. Here's a guide to some of Route 66's most breathtaking scenic routes and natural wonders:

Illinois

- **Shawnee National Forest**

Route: From Chicago, travel Interstate 55 South to the Shawnee National Forest. From there, take IL-146 eastward. The forest is situated 150 miles from St. Louis in southern Illinois.

How to Get There: Take IL-146 east after traveling south on I-55 from the Springfield interchange of Route 66 and Interstate 55. Pay attention to the Shawnee National Forest signage.

Why It's Unique: Compared to Chicago's urban surroundings, the Shawnee National Forest offers a striking shift in view. This 280,000-acre forest is renowned for its breathtaking views, rich woods, and impressive rock formations. The Garden of the Gods, with its striking rock formations and expansive views, and the Little Grand Canyon, which provides a rough, canyon-like experience, are two of the area's main attractions. There are fantastic hiking, birdwatching, and photography opportunities in the forest.

Missouri

- **Ozark National Scenic Riverways**

Route: Take Interstate 44 west from St. Louis to US-63 south. The riverways are close to the town of Van Buren in southern Missouri.

How to Get There: From St. Louis, take I-44 west, and then US-63 south. To reach the Ozark National Scenic Riverways, follow the signage.

Why It's Unique: The Current and Jacks Fork Rivers, which are well-known for their crystal-clear, spring-fed waters and breathtaking landscape, are safeguarded by the Ozark National Scenic Riverways. Fishing, kayaking, and canoeing are all excellent here. Views of undulating hills, limestone cliffs, and lush forests can be seen on the picturesque drives through the Ozarks. The Alley Spring Mill and Big Spring are only two of the important areas of interest that can be reached on the picturesque trip along Highway 19. Don't miss it.

Oklahoma

- **Red Rock Canyon**

Route: Travel west on Interstate 44 from Oklahoma City to Hydro, then west on US-62. The canyon is roughly ninety miles from Oklahoma City, close to Hydro, Oklahoma.

How to Get There: From Oklahoma City, head west on I-44 and then west on US-62 to the town of Hydro. See the directions for Red Rock Canyon.

Why It's Unique: The sandstone rocks at Red Rock Canyon are a stunning red and orange color that contrasts with the surrounding plains environment. There are breathtaking views of the canyon from picnic areas, hiking paths, and scenic drives in the vicinity. A gorgeous waterfall and several well-liked rock formations by rock climbers may also be found in the park. Driving down the canyon offers a distinctive viewpoint of the splendor of Oklahoma's natural surroundings.

Texas

- **Palo Duro Canyon**

Route: Travel east on US-84 from Amarillo to the Palo Duro Canyon State Park gate.

How to Get There: Take US-84 east from Amarillo. To reach Palo Duro Canyon State Park, follow the signage.

Why It's Unique: Palo Duro Canyon, the second-largest canyon in the country, is referred to as the "Grand Canyon of Texas." The park is home to a variety of wildlife species, wide-open spaces, and striking red rock formations. The park's scenic roads provide amazing views of the deep ravines and stratified rock formations of the canyon. Hiking paths that offer up-close views of the geological features of the canyon include the Lighthouse Trail. Additionally, the park is home to the outdoor musical spectacle "Texas," which highlights the history and culture of the area.

New Mexico

- **Sandia Crest Scenic Byway**

Route: Head north on NM-14 from Albuquerque to NM-536, which takes you to Sandia Crest.

How to Get There: Take NM-14 north out of Albuquerque and turn onto NM-536. To get to the Sandia Crest parking lot, follow the road.

Why It's Unique: Offering a breathtaking journey from the desert bottom to the summit of the Sandia Mountains, the Sandia Crest Scenic Byway offers breathtaking panoramic views of Albuquerque and the surrounding desert scenery. You will pass through a variety of environments during the route, including lush alpine woodland and parched desert. Visitors can take advantage of expansive vistas, hiking trails, and chances to see wildlife at the peak. The Sandia Crest is especially breathtaking in the morning and evening.

Arizona

- **The Painted Desert**

Route: Head north on US-89 to the Painted Desert Visitor Center from Flagstaff.

Directions: From Flagstaff, take US-89 north to the Painted Desert Visitor Center. To reach the several paths and overlooks in the Painted Desert, follow the signage.

Why It's Unique: Wide-ranging vistas and colorful, multicolored rock formations are the highlights of the Painted Desert. The red, orange, and purple tones of the desert stand out strikingly against the blue sky. The distinctive geology and vibrant landscape can be explored by tourists via scenic drives and walking routes. One of the main attractions is the Petrified Forest National Park, where visitors may witness remarkable geological formations and ancient petrified wood.

California

- **Route 66 through the Mojave Desert**

Route: Take I-40 west from Kingman, AZ to the Mojave National Preserve.

How to Get There: From Kingman, follow I-40 west and exit at Mojave National Preserve. To get to the preserve's main features, follow the signage.

Why It's Unique: California's distinctive geological characteristics and desert vegetation are highlighted by the Mojave Desert, which offers a harsh yet stunning landscape. Key stops include the Kelso Dunes, the Kelso Depot, and the Mojave's Joshua Trees. Views of expansive, open landscapes and striking mountain backdrops can be seen during the picturesque trip through the desert. The desert is a particularly remarkable section of the Route 66 journey because of its isolation and vast views.

These outdoor pursuits along Route 66 provide a wide range of picturesque drives and natural wonders that enhance Mother Road's historic and cultural attractions. Every location offers chances for exploration and adventure as well as a distinctive look at America's natural splendor.

Parks and Recreational Areas

Beyond its historic sites and oddball roadside attractions, Route 66 includes a variety of parks and recreational spaces where visitors may engage in outdoor activities, take in the scenery, and get away from the hustle and bustle of the road. The following is a list of some of the top parks and leisure spots along the Mother Road:

Illinois

- **Kickapoo State Park**

Location: Oakwood, Illinois, three miles southeast

Route & Directions: Take Interstate 55 South out of Chicago and merge onto Interstate 74 West. Follow the signs to Kickapoo State Park after leaving at Oakwood.

Why It's Unique: Tucked among lush forests and rolling hills lies Kickapoo State Park, which has a variety of hiking paths, picnic spaces, and fishing spots. In addition to a 20-acre lake for boating and fishing, the park has more than 20 miles of hiking and mountain bike paths. It's a tranquil getaway that offers a refreshing change of scenery from Chicago's busy city.

Missouri

- **Forest Park**

Location: Missouri's St. Louis

Directions and How to Get There: Go northeast to Forest Park from St. Louis' Route 66. Major St. Louis roadways provide easy access to the park due to its central location.

Why It's Unique: With a multitude of recreational opportunities and sights to see, Forest Park is one of the biggest urban parks in the country. The park has routes for bicyclists and walkers, a golf course, and several cultural establishments, such as the Missouri History Museum, the Art Museum, and the St. Louis Zoo. It's a terrific place to explore and unwind because of its vast green spaces and picturesque surroundings.

Oklahoma

- **Oxley Nature Center**

Location: Near the Oxley Nature Center and Tulsa Zoo in Tulsa, Oklahoma

Directions & How to Get There: Take Memorial Drive north from Tulsa's Route 66. To get to Oxley Nature Center and the Tulsa Zoo, follow the signage.

Why It's Unique: The Oxley Nature Center provides a unique combination of outdoor learning and pleasure in a natural environment. The site offers hiking routes that pass through prairies, wetlands, and forests, among other types of habitat. It also offers educational sessions about the area's flora and fauna, as well as opportunities to see wildlife. The Tulsa Zoo is close by, making the center an ideal place to stop for a full day of outdoor activities.

Texas

- **Palo Duro Canyon State Park**

Location: Close to Canyon, Texas

Route & Directions: Travel east on US-84 from Amarillo to the Palo Duro Canyon State Park gate.

Why It's Unique: Offering a variety of outdoor activities and stunning scenery, Palo Duro Canyon is the second-largest canyon in the United States. The park offers beautiful drives with breathtaking views of the multicolored rock formations of the canyon, hiking trails, and horseback riding. Additionally, the park is home to the outdoor musical spectacle "Texas," which honors the history and culture of the area.

New Mexico

- **Petroglyph National Monument**

Location: New Mexico's Albuquerque

Directions & How to Get There: The Petroglyph National Monument can be reached by heading west on Western Trail from Route 66 in Albuquerque and following the signs.

Why It's Unique: A sizable collection of prehistoric rock engravings created by Native Americans and early Spanish settlers is preserved at Petroglyph National Monument. The monument offers several pathways where visitors can get up close and personal with these petroglyphs, giving them an insight into the historical and cultural legacy of the area. Hikes in the park are picturesque and offer expansive views of the surrounding desert scenery and the Albuquerque Basin.

Arizona

- **Grand Canyon National Park**

Location: Williams, Arizona, to the north

Directions and How to Get There: The Grand Canyon National Park may be reached straight from Kingman by taking I-40 East to US-64 North.

Why It's Unique: The Grand Canyon, one of nature's most famous wonders, provides vistas of its vast and vibrant terrain that are unmatched. The park offers hiking paths like the Bright Angel Trail in addition to several overlooks, including the North and South Rims. The canyon can be explored on foot, by bicycle, or even from the air with a helicopter trip that offers an amazing view.

California

- **Joshua Tree National Park**

Location: Close to California's Twentynine Palms

Route & Directions: Take I-40 West out of Barstow to Highway 62, then follow the directions to Joshua Tree National Park.

Why It's Unique: Named for its namesake Joshua trees, dramatic rock formations, and expansive open areas, Joshua Tree National Park is well-known for its distinctive desert vistas. Numerous outdoor pursuits are available at the park, such as rock climbing, hiking, and stargazing. Skull Rock, Barker Dam, and Hidden Valley are among the notable locations. Nature lovers should not miss the park because of its unique ecosystems and bizarre landscape.

A range of outdoor activities are available at these parks and recreation sites, including hiking, wildlife viewing, scenic drives, and cultural exploration. Whether you're looking for scenic views, educational opportunities, or just a place to relax, these Route 66 locations are the ideal addition to your travel experiences.

Chapter 9. Local Culture and Festivals

Annual Events and Celebrations

One of the best ways to get fully immersed in the atmosphere of the adventure is to take in the local customs and festivals while traveling along Route 66. Through yearly celebrations and festivals that provide a sample of regional customs, cuisine, and entertainment, each region honors its heritage. Here is a schedule of some of the major yearly gatherings and festivities that you can take part in along the famous route:

Illinois

- **Route 66 Festival**

Dates: 2024 June 14–16

Where: Springfield, Illinois

Why Go: With live music, vintage car shows, and a wide range of food vendors, this festival honors the rich history and culture of Route 66. Highlights include historical reenactments that capture the essence of the Mother Road and vintage automobile parades. It's a great chance to interact with fans of Route 66 and take in the lively local scene.

Details: The festival is held in Springfield's downtown, which makes it convenient to see nearby sights and restaurants. Local bands usually perform at the event, and there are also unique exhibits on the history of Route 66.

Missouri

- **St. Louis International Film Festival**

Dates: 2024 November 7–17

Location: Missouri's St. Louis

Why Attend: Independent and foreign films from all around the world are featured at the St. Louis International Film Festival. It's a fantastic chance to take in St. Louis' vibrant cultural scene and watch movies that would not be shown in conventional theaters. For those who love movies, the festival offers panel discussions, screenings, and chances to network.

Details: There are several sites in St. Louis' downtown. Deep dives into the realm of cinema are offered by the festival's special events and Q&A sessions with filmmakers.

Oklahoma

- **Tulsa International Mayfest**

Dates: 16–19 May, 2024

Location: Oklahoma's Tulsa

Why Go: Held in downtown Tulsa, Tulsa International Mayfest is a lively celebration of music, art, and crafts. The event offers a variety of artisan stalls, local cuisine from food sellers, and musical performances by both national and local artists. There are family-friendly events, interactive installations, and art displays for people of all ages.

Details: The festival, which takes place in the center of Tulsa's Arts District, offers a chance to take in live entertainment and peruse neighborhood galleries. The event is a fantastic way to get a sense of Tulsa's creative culture.

Texas

- **Amarillo Route 66 Motor Show**

Dates: 2024 September 13–15

Place: Texas's Amarillo

Why Go: With a variety of antique vehicles on exhibit, this yearly motor show honors the heritage of Route 66 and classic cars. Live music, food trucks, and an automobile cruise are all part of the event. For those who enjoy cars and the nostalgia of Route 66, it's a must-visit.

Specifics: The performance happens at the Amarillo Civic Center among other places in the city. The occasion offers a lively, family-friendly setting with lots of chances for mingling and taking pictures.

New Mexico

- **Albuquerque International Balloon Fiesta**

Dates: 2024 October 5–13

Location: New Mexico's Albuquerque

Why Go: Drawing tourists from all over the world, the Albuquerque International Balloon Fiesta is the biggest hot-air balloon festival in the world. Hundreds of balloons will take to the air as part of the festival, along with balloon glows at night and unique shapes. It's an amazing visual extravaganza and a singular way to take in Albuquerque's dynamic culture.

Information: Balloon Fiesta Park is the venue for the fiesta. The festival features live music, food vendors, and cultural exhibits in addition to balloon launches. Enjoying Albuquerque's natural beauty and sense of community is a terrific opportunity.

Arizona

- **Route 66 Fun Run**

Dates: 3–5 May 2024

Location: Arizona, between Kingman to Oatman

Why Go: Every year, admirers of Route 66, motorcyclists, and enthusiasts of vintage cars get together for the Route 66 Fun Run. During the run, antique cars parade down Route 66, stopping in several communities for events and festivities. It's an opportunity to honor the history of Route 66 and unite with a community of enthusiasts.

Specifics: Oatman is where the event concludes after it begins in Kingman. Visitors take pleasure in historical exhibits, live music, and picturesque driving. For those who wish to feel the thrill and camaraderie of the Route 66 community, the Fun Run is a highlight.

California

- **Santa Monica Pier Twilight Concerts**

June through August of the year 2024

Where: Santa Monica, California

Why Go: The renowned Santa Monica Pier hosts a series of free outdoor concerts known as the "Twilight Concerts." A wide range of musical acts, including both well-known performers and local bands, are scheduled for the events. It's a great way to listen to music and enjoy the sights of Santa Monica Beach and the Pacific Ocean.

Information: Tickets are available for the concerts on a first-come, first-served basis at the pier's stage. The event is ideal for an evening of entertainment by the water and offers a laid-back vibe.

A great way to enhance your road trip experience is through these festivals and events along Route 66, which provide insight into the customs and culture of the area. Every occasion offers a different opportunity to interact with the local people along the route and commemorate the rich history of this famous highway.

Cultural Highlights Along Route 66

Discovering the diverse cultural fabric of America while driving along Route 66 is an experience beyond the breathtaking scenery and well-known sites. From thriving art scenes to historical buildings that chronicle the American experience, every area along this historic road provides distinctive cultural experiences. The following is a list of some of the major cultural attractions you can see along the way:

Chicago, Illinois – The Birthplace of Route 66

- **The Art Institute of Chicago**

Where: 111 S. Avenue Michigan, Chicago, IL

Why Go: The Art Institute of Chicago is home to one of the biggest and oldest collections of artwork in the country, which includes works of art by renowned artists including Grant Wood and Georges Seurat. Its famous architecture and varied exhibits offer a comprehensive look into Chicago's and other cities' creative histories.

Details: The museum hosts a variety of exhibitions, educational activities, and special events. It is a prominent cultural institution in Chicago. Adult admission costs roughly $25.

St. Louis, Missouri: A Cultural Crossroads

- **The Gateway Arch**

Location: St. Louis, MO; 100 Washington Avenue

Why Go: The Gateway Arch is a potent representation of American history and westward migration. A tram trip up the Arch will provide visitors sweeping views of the city and the Mississippi River; alternatively, they can explore the museum at its base to discover more about the history of the American frontier.

Details: The museum at the top of the iconic St. Louis skyline, the Arch, features displays about the history of westward migration and the influence of St. Louis on the formation of the United States.

- **The Delmar Loop**

Location: St. Louis, Missouri's Delmar Boulevard

Why Visit: With a wide selection of eateries, stores, and entertainment options, this diverse neighborhood is well-known for its thriving cultural scene. Street art, live music, and cultural festivals abound around the Delmar Loop, which is a creative hotspot that captures the vibrant energy of St. Louis.

Details: The St. Louis Walk of Fame, which honors famous citizens of the city, is located in the Loop. It's a fantastic place to eat, see live entertainment, and learn about local culture.

Tulsa, Oklahoma – A Cultural Gem

- **Philbrook Museum of Art**

Address: 2727 S. OK's Rockford Road, Tulsa

Why Go: The Philbrook Museum of Art has an amazing collection of American, European, and modern art and is housed in a stunning Italianate home. In the center of Tulsa, the museum's breathtaking gardens and changing displays offer a diverse cultural experience.

Details: The museum is well-known for both its promotion of Oklahoma's artistic community and its carefully planned displays. Adult admission is approximately $10.

- **Greenwood District**

Location: Tulsa, Oklahoma, Greenwood Avenue

Why Go: Known by many as Black Wall Street or the Greenwood District, this historic neighborhood is well-known for its important role in African American history. Before the racial massacre in 1921, the neighborhood was a bustling business center. With museums and memorials that pay tribute to its heritage, it functions as a historical and cultural hub today.

Details: Learning about the history of the district and its effects on the neighborhood may be gained by visiting the John Hope Franklin Reconciliation Park and the Greenwood Cultural Center.

Santa Fe, New Mexico – A Blend of Tradition and Innovation

- **Santa Fe Plaza**

Place: Plaza, New Mexico's Santa Fe

Why Visit: Encircled by galleries, museums, and ancient buildings, the Santa Fe Plaza is the city's historic center. Visitors can explore Spanish colonial history, contemporary artistic expressions, and traditional Native American art at this dynamic cultural hub.

Details: A variety of cultural events, such as art markets, festivals, and performances, are held at The Plaza. You can learn a lot about the history, gastronomy, and art of the area there.

- **Georgia O'Keeffe Museum**

Location: Santa Fe, New Mexico; 217 Johnson Street

Why Go: This museum, which honors the works of the well-known artist Georgia O'Keeffe, features her famous paintings as well as information about her life and creative process. O'Keeffe's art is closely associated with the topography and traditions of New Mexico.

Details: A variety of exhibitions, educational activities, and special events are available at the museum. Adult admission fees are about $12.

Kingman, Arizona – Route 66 Hub

- **Route 66 Museum**

120 W is the location. Arizona's Andy Devine Avenue, Kingman

Why Go: The Route 66 Museum in Kingman offers a comprehensive look at the history and cultural significance of Route 66. It is housed within the Mohave Museum of History and Arts. Vintage signs, pictures, and memorabilia from the Mother Road's heyday are on display.

Details: The museum provides an in-depth examination of Route 66's past, emphasizing both its impact on the growth of the West and its relevance in American society.

Santa Monica, California – The End of the Road

- **Santa Monica Pier**

At Santa Monica Pier in Santa Monica, California

Why Go: The Santa Monica Pier, a historic monument with a variety of attractions like restaurants, an aquarium, and an amusement park, is located near the western end of Route 66. The pier, a thriving cultural hub, is a wonderful way to end the Route 66 adventure.

Details: In addition to the famous Ferris wheel and seasonal events, the pier offers a variety of entertainment options. It is a well-liked location for both locals and tourists, providing beautiful scenery and a lively environment.

The many customs, historical events, and artistic manifestations that can be discovered along Route 66 are glimpsed through these cultural highlights. Every location offers a distinctive experience that enhances your travel by giving you a greater appreciation for the history of this famous highway and the essence of America.

Chapter 10. Practical Information

Traveling on Route 66 necessitates thorough planning and preparation. This comprehensive guide will assist you in making the most of your journey, from figuring out the best routes to handling traffic and making sure your car runs well.

Navigational Hints

Planning Your Route

The distance on Route 66 from Chicago, Illinois, to Santa Monica, California, is roughly 2,448 miles. You will travel through eight states on the route, each with its special attractions and experiences. To successfully navigate the route:

- **Utilize a Reliable Map or GPS:** Although a large portion of Route 66 is signposted, staying on course can be ensured by using a GPS or a thorough map. Additionally, there are applications and maps specifically designed for Route 66 that highlight important landmarks and historical sites.
- **Follow Route 66 Markers**: Keep an eye out for the recognizable "Route 66" signs and shields. You can stay on the historic walk and avoid getting lost by following these markings.

Major Driving Segments

Here's a breakdown of key driving segments along Route 66:

- **Chicago, IL to St. Louis, MO (Approx. 300 miles):** This segment covers urban landscapes and historic small towns. The drive generally takes 5 to 6 hours without stops.
- **St. Louis, MO to Springfield, MO (Approx. 100 miles):** Expect a journey of about 2 hours, featuring a mix of historic towns and scenic landscapes.
- **Springfield, MO to Tulsa, OK (Approx. 220 miles):** This drive takes around 4 hours and includes both rural areas and vibrant cities.
- **Tulsa, OK to Amarillo, TX (Approx. 330 miles):** A longer drive of approximately 5 to 6 hours, passing through diverse landscapes and interesting stops.
- **Amarillo, TX to Santa Fe, NM (Approx. 290 miles):** Expect around 5 hours of driving through the arid landscapes of the Southwest.
- **Santa Fe, NM to Kingman, AZ (Approx. 420 miles):** This is one of the longer stretches, taking about 7 to 8 hours, and includes both desert scenery and historic sites.
- **Kingman, AZ to Santa Monica, CA (Approx. 300 miles):** The final leg, taking around 5 to 6 hours, ends at the iconic Santa Monica Pier.

Weather and Road Conditions

- **Weather Considerations**: There are several different climates along Route 66. Be ready for scorching weather in the desert, chilly weather at higher altitudes, and possibly rainy weather in some places. Regularly check the weather forecast and schedule your stops appropriately.

- **Road Conditions**: Although Route 66 is mostly paved, there may be some unpaved or unfinished areas. Use caution when driving and be ready for uneven or detourous terrain.

Driving Advice

Vehicle Preparation

- **Examine Your Car**: Before leaving on a trip, make sure your car is in good operating order. Examine the brakes, tires, oil, and other vital components. Pre-trip inspections can guarantee trouble-free travel and help avoid problems.
- Put together an emergency kit by gathering supplies including a spare tire, jack, jumper cables, basic tools, first aid kit, and flashlight.

Gas and Rest Areas

- **Refuel Often**: Although there are plenty of petrol stations along Route 66, there may be less throughout sections of its length, especially in rural areas. To prevent running out of gas, keep your tank full and fill up whenever you can.
- **Take Breaks**: Long drives can be exhausting. Schedule regular stops along the trip to visit interesting locations, stretch your legs, and grab a bite to eat.

Recommendations

- **Plan Ahead**: Securing lodging in advance will help you avoid last-minute searches and guarantee a place to stay, especially during popular travel seasons. Seek

lodging establishments along Route 66 that have a nostalgic feel.
- **Explore Unique Stays**: For a genuinely genuine experience, think about booking a room at a historic inn or one of the famous Route 66 motels. These lodgings frequently have a charming, old-world feel to them.

Etiquette and Safety

- **Observe Traffic Laws**: Drive defensively and by applicable local laws. Certain regions could have particular speed restrictions or traffic laws.
- **Respect Local Communities**: A lot of small towns and rural areas are traversed along Route 66. Along the trip, show your support for regional companies and abide by the customs and traditions of the area.

Navigational Aids

- **Use Apps and Guides**: A plethora of Route 66 applications and guidebooks are available, including comprehensive details about lodgings, dining options, and attractions. You can find hidden gems and improve your experience with these resources.
- **Download Offline Maps**: Along Route 66, cellular coverage is not always consistent. To make sure you can get navigational information even when there is no service, download offline maps or guides.

This driving and navigational advice will put you in a good position to have a smooth and enjoyable trip down the iconic Route 66. Happy travels!

Safety and Local Etiquette

Traveling Route 66 is an exciting historical and exploratory excursion. Being ready and honoring local norms are crucial for a safe and pleasurable vacation. This information will assist you in navigating local etiquette and safety problems.

Emergency Contacts and Services

Emergency Contacts:

- **Police, Fire, and Medical Emergencies:** Dial 911 for all emergencies, including police, fire, and medical situations.
- **Roadside Assistance:**
    - **AAA (American Automobile Association):** Call 1-800-AAA-HELP (1-800-222-4357) for roadside assistance, including towing, battery jumps, and lockout services.
    - **Roadside Assistance Programs:** Many credit cards and car insurance policies offer roadside assistance. Check your policy details for specific contact information.
- **Poison Control:** For poison-related emergencies, call the National Capital Poison Center at 1-800-222-1222.
- **Non-Emergency Police Contact:**
    - **Chicago Police Department:** 312-746-6000
    - **St. Louis Metropolitan Police Department:** 314-231-1212
    - **Oklahoma City Police Department:** 405-231-2121

- Los Angeles Police Department: 213-486-6911
- **Local Hospitals and Urgent Care:**
  - **Chicago:** Northwestern Memorial Hospital, 312-926-2000
  - **St. Louis:** Barnes-Jewish Hospital, 314-747-3000
  - **Oklahoma City:** OU Medical Center, 405-271-4340
  - **Los Angeles:** Cedars-Sinai Medical Center, 310-659-5500

Safety Tips

Be Ready for Any Weather Situations:

- **Check Weather Forecast**: Along Route 66, there might be considerable variations in the weather. In particular in arid areas, be ready for storms, sudden downpours, and extremely high or low temperatures by routinely checking the weather.
- **Carry the necessities**: To stay hydrated and shield yourself from the sun, bring plenty of drink, sunscreen, a hat, and sunglasses.

Car Security:

- **Maintain Your Car**: Before leaving on a trip, make sure your car is in good working order. Breakdowns can be avoided with routine maintenance, such as monitoring tire pressure and oil levels.
- **Emergency Kit**: Keep a basic tools kit, first aid kit, flashlight, jack, spare tire, and jumper cables in your car.

Remain Alert:

- **Lock Your Car:** To deter theft, always lock your car's doors and keep valuables hidden.
- **Be Aware of Your Surroundings**: Be cautious in strange places and steer clear of dangerous districts, especially after dark.

Health Guard Measures:

- **Keep Yourself Hydrated**: Avoid dehydration by drinking lots of water, especially in warm regions.
- **Food Safety**: Use caution when consuming food and beverages, especially when visiting unfamiliar locations. Make sure the meal is cooked all the way through and the drinks come from reliable suppliers.

Local Etiquette

Respect Local Customs:

- **Respect Local Laws**: Observe traffic laws, local ordinances, and codes of conduct. This involves abiding by noise and speed restrictions.
- **Greet Locals Politely**: A welcoming attitude and courteous salutations go a long way. It can be nice to hear basic expressions like "hello" or "thank you" in regional accents.

Support Local Businesses:

- **Shop Locally**: Support small businesses and local vendors along Route 66. They frequently sell one-of-a-kind goods and mementos.

- **Give A Generous Tipping**: It is common to leave a tip of 15-20% at restaurants and service establishments. In larger gatherings especially, be sure the gratuity is included by always checking the bill.

Environmental Responsibility:

- **Get Rid of Trash Correctly**: Preserve the environment by putting rubbish in the appropriate bins and recycling whatever you can.
- Respect nature by leaving it as you found it, adhering to trail signs, and keeping animals at bay when visiting parks and natural areas.

Cultural Sensitivity:

- **Respect Historical places**: Keep in mind the importance of historical places when you visit museums and landmarks. Observe any posted policies and directives.
- **Recognize Local Traditions**: Every location may have its own set of traditions and customs. To guarantee a good rapport with the local community, observe and respect these customs.

Conclusion

You may find yourself thinking back on the many miles you've driven, the diverse range of scenery you've encountered, and the rich experiences this fabled route has to offer as the sun sets on your Route 66 journey. Route 66 is more than just a route; it's a trip through the heart of America, a story imprinted in memory and asphalt, from the busy streets of Chicago to the golden coastlines of Santa Monica.

I sincerely hope this book has brightened your way and enhanced your experience when you reflect on your adventures. Every chapter and suggestion was written to assist you in discovering the charm of Route 66, highlighting its well-known sites, and exposing its best-kept secrets. I hope the stories in these pages have strengthened your bond with this legendary route, whether you traveled through quaint eateries, marveled at historical sites, or just took in the open road.

I'd be interested in learning how this book has affected your travels, as your trip down Route 66 is a special chapter in your narrative. Did it take you to some cute little roadside spot that you might have missed otherwise? Was there a hidden gem or a local favorite that became a highlight of your trip? Your knowledge and experiences are priceless, and by sharing them, we can assist other travelers who are planning to take their own Route 66 trips.

If you would want to discuss how this book benefited you along the path, please consider posting a review. Your suggestions not only help me get better, but they also help other people plan their amazing trip down Main Street America.

Remember that Route 66 is more than simply a place to travel; it's a celebration of the American spirit, a monument to the delights of adventure, and a constant reminder of the limitless opportunities that lay just beyond the horizon as you consider the miles you've traveled and the tales you've gathered. May your path always rise to meet you, and safe travels.

Made in the USA
Monee, IL
14 November 2024